Emil Schulthess   Soviet Union

Emil Schulthess

Sovi

Commentary by Harrison E. Salisbury

its automobile industry. A *kolkhoz* of cosmic dimensions farms the fertile soil mechanically, yet small family gardens exist with proportionately much higher yields than those of the state and collective farms. While cosmonauts are rocketed into space in Baykonyr, housewives in Siberia draw water for the kitchen from wells in their backyards. The Tu-144, the newest commercial aircraft in the U.S.S.R., runs test flights high above the Siberian expanses at twice the speed of sound, while down below trappers pull their crude sleds through the taiga. Prodigious is the area of the Soviet Union; vast are the distances. The United States fits into the territory of the U.S.S.R. three times; France, the largest Western European nation, a full forty times. The country stretches across 170° of longitude from west to east, encompassing close to half the northern hemisphere of our globe. When of a summer evening the sun sinks below the horizon on the western borders, it is simultaneously rising to greet the following day on the eastern borders — the Soviet Union is the only land where the sun never sets.

I became acquainted with the Soviet Union for the first time some forty years ago through *UdSSR im Bau*, a magazine that circulated at the art school in Zurich where I was studying applied art. As "disciples of the fine arts", we were impressed by the fact that the Soviet Union — the country that had attained a new social order — was in the avant-garde with respect to art, cinema, photography, and architecture and that such advanced designers as Le Corbusier were consulted on questions of national development projects and city planning. We may have had little sympathy with or understanding of the new ideals and the ideologies of Marx and Lenin, but we greatly admired the recent achievements of industrialization — the first tractor to roll off the assembly line in 1930, the first diesel locomotive on rails a year later, or the ambitious plans for the Dnieper power plant. Not until I began planning a photographic documentary of the U.S.S.R. just a few years ago did I actually come into direct contact with the Soviet Union and its inhabitants. Having already published several photographic works on other parts of the world, I was very eager to compile a pictorial image of the U.S.S.R., a perplexing country, so admired by some, so feared by others. This country was to come to life not only in its "Sunday best", as it always seems to have been presented, but also as it appears every day, including, perhaps, its less pleasant aspects as well as its pleasant ones. It was clear from the very beginning that such an undertaking could succeed only if I were allowed to travel not merely to those regions accessible through Intourist, the government travel agency, but also to regions that had thus far been closed to tourists and to Western reporters. To this end I worked out a proposal that included practical suggestions for carrying out the undertaking as well as my more general ideas for the composition of a photographic volume.

As early as 1960, Alfred Zehnder, who was then the Swiss ambassador to Moscow, had submitted my plans to the Soviet Ministry of Culture. Four years later I called on the press attaché of the Soviet Embassy in Bern and requested that he also direct my proposal to Moscow. In November 1966 I discussed the project with August Lindt, a new ambassador who had been appointed to Moscow, and just two months later I received a telegram inviting me to travel to Moscow for initial exploratory talks. The authorities expressed interest in my plans. Although no definite promises were made, the meeting in Moscow gave me reason to hope that a photographic treatment of restricted areas was not altogether impossible. I did, however, categorically refuse the offer of already existing pictures or of photographs that the Soviets themselves would take in restricted areas and make available for my exclusive use.

It was obvious from the beginning that I would never be allowed to travel through districts that were closed to Soviet citizens themselves. Thus, there was no point in trying to obtain a permit to visit the Cosmodrome in Baykonyr. No Western journalist has ever been allowed to witness the launching of a Soviet spacecraft; in fact, Charles de Gaulle and Georges Pompidou are the only Western statesmen ever invited to the spaceport. Years ago an American magazine had offered — in vain — $1 million for the right to visit and photograph Baykonyr. Nevertheless, I always carried a Leica motor with me just in case an unexpected opportunity would develop for me to film the swift sequence of a rocket as it is being launched from the pad. I still keep this equipment ready for action, should, one day, an invitation to Baykonyr come through after all.

Far more patience, time, and money were required for this project than for any of the previous ones. The correspondence, proposed schedules, itineraries, and lists that I sent to Moscow in the preliminary stages fill a thick file. Had I at that time had any idea how difficult it would be to realize my plans, I should probably never have ventured more than the first trip. Constant setbacks that obstructed the goal finally discouraged me, and I was ready to give up the undertaking altogether. One day I returned to my hotel utterly dejected in the company of a Soviet journalist who had been taking part in the negotiations. He tried to cheer me up and offered to assist me in overcoming some of the obstacles and difficulties that were holding things up. When I finally decided that I would proceed with the project, Oleg, as he was called, became my irreplaceable companion. He helped make travel arrangements in Moscow, sought special permits, assisted my work in every way during our trips together and, in addition to all this, acted as my interpreter. Despite his energy and good will, we still often found ourselves faced with unexpected obstacles and met occasionally by lack of understanding, indifference, and suspicion. Although Oleg and I do not think alike in many respects — Oleg is a Soviet citizen, a convinced Communist, and an admirer of Lenin — we grew very close during our travels; we have become fast friends.

Finally, after seven journeys to the Soviet Union, I had 8,000 pictures to work with in putting together this volume. Any attempt at photographic documentation of this immense many-faceted nation is necessarily fragmentary. Furthermore, the basic conception underlying my plans was very difficult to execute in view of the constant alterations in travel arrangements. A photographic work on the Soviet Union, no matter how carefully planned and prepared, is occasionally at the mercy of chance; yet, in a very special way, it will or can become a personal statement. I therefore felt it important not merely to present a sequence of pictures but to complement them with my own commentary. Wherever possible in the course of my travels, I endeavored to collect and evaluate factual information, some of which may, of course, also be available elsewhere. However, my principal aim has been to impart not political or general observations but rather personal impressions in order to give a full and vivid account of what I have seen. For this, the American edition, Harrison E. Salisbury of the *New York Times* has written a Commentary. Mr. Salisbury did not travel with me and our views of Russian history and Soviet society differ in many respects. Nevertheless, as a longtime student of the Soviet Union he offers many special insights.

West of the Urals

The external circumstances did not lend themselves to this self-imposed task. My visits to the Soviet Union extended over a period of four years, beginning during the "thaw" when for the first time Western newspapers and other publications were appearing on newsstands in Soviet hotels and continuing long after Soviet troops had marched into Czechoslovakia. It is therefore not surprising that I found myself somewhat torn in the course of observing and getting to know the Soviet Union and that the country remains for me an enigmatic entity, a sphinx, capable of great achievements in the technical world, able to explore the surface of the moon with a remote-control lunar probe, and yet unable to satisfy basic needs of the man in the street.

A documentary on the Soviet Union which presented a glorified view of the land and its people and described only its spectacular technical achievements would do as little justice to the truth as an account which overemphasized the negative aspects of life and conditions in the U.S.S.R.

This volume of photographs is divided into three sections: the first deals with the U.S.S.R. to the west of the Ural Mountains, the second with the Central Asian republics, and the third with Siberia. To gather the material for this book, I made seven journeys to the Soviet Union during which I covered more than 30,000 miles by plane, rail, four-wheel-drive vehicles in rugged terrain, and a variety of boats. I undertook the greater part of the journey through western Russia, with which this book begins, in my own car.

Oleg and I had agreed by telephone to meet at 8 A.M. on a certain day at Chop on the Russian-Hungarian border. (Chop is the gateway to the Ukraine, the crossroads for automobile and rail traffic alike, with direct connections to Moscow and Kiev and to Prague, Budapest, Sofia, Vienna, and other southeastern European cities.) In my heavily loaded vehicle I drove on the throughway from Ulm via Munich to Vienna, then through Budapest and on almost to the Russian border, where I stopped for the night. I reached Hungarian customs early the next day. No other traveler was to be seen crossing the border. After thoroughly searching my car, the customs officials waved me on to the Russian side, where passport and vehicle were checked first. While my photographic books, papers, and letters of recommendation were all being scrutinized, I was called to the telephone. Oleg. He had just arrived at the Chop railway station and would be at the border in about half an hour.

By the time Oleg arrived — to my surprise with a perfectly clean-shaven head — all the formalities had been completed. He had been looking forward to our trip and was delighted with my car, a new Citroën DS-21. We collected his luggage at the station and got under way.

Chop — Uzhgorod — Lvov — Kiev

The weather could not have been more perfect. We first drove through the Carpathians, which reminded me of northeastern Switzerland. Then the landscape flattened out as we approached the grain-growing country of the Ukraine.

1 *Road between Chop and Kiev.* The road here rises and falls endlessly. We were slowed down by trucks, which filled the road, especially near the larger cities. Passing them was out of the question since we could never see far enough ahead because of the dips in the road. Multilane highways do not exist in the Soviet Union.

2 *Landscape between Uzhgorod and Zhitomir.* Plains are the dominant feature of the Ukrainian landscape; wheat fields stretch all the way to the horizon. It was the middle of July and hot. There had been no rain for weeks; the roads and lanes were ankle-deep in dust.
We visited the "Twenty-second Party Day" Collective Farm, run by Ivan Kolka, a pleasant man of about forty. The 1,800 farms in the collective total about 12,350 acres, planted mainly with wheat. We spent the night here so that we would be able to watch the harvesting the next day. Although we could have slept in my car, which was equipped for this purpose, the manager of the collective offered us a room next to his office.
Early the next morning we drove out to the six monstrous harvesting machines, the combines, which had already harvested a a good part of the vast wheat field.

3 *Harvesters at work at the "Twenty-second Party Day" Collective Farm.* Unfortunately, there was no rise in the ground from which one could overlook the great expanse of wheat fields. Oleg hoisted me onto his shoulders, enabling me to get a shot from above.
The dust was a plague. Our car creaked and squeaked in every joint. Besides, while driving across the field, I ran over some ob-

struction that dented the car, and now the wheels made a loud scraping noise every time I turned them. We took the car into a workshop for farm machinery. In no time at all we were surrounded by curious onlookers.
No one had ever seen such a car! A mechanic finally started to work on it. After examining the damage, he asked Oleg if we had a "Catholic screwdriver" in our toolbox, meaning one that is shaped like a cross on top. In less than an hour the car was repaired — and washed. The whole job cost 3 rubles, a little over $ 3.00. We continued our trip.

4 *Center of Lvov (Lemberg) with a film poster in the background.* Lvov is a major cultural and industrial center of the western Ukraine. Not only are there machine, appliance, and automobile factories, but also electrical, electronic, and chemical industries. More than 60,000 students are registered at the various colleges and universities. The city has a population of 553,000.

5 *Gas station sign outside Kiev.* The Western motorist soon realizes that gas stations in the Soviet Union are rare indeed. Between the border and Moscow they are sometimes as much as 60 miles apart, usually located near an intersection on the outskirts of a city. Since service stations have neither billboards nor neon lights, they are called to the motorist's attention by these signs placed alongside the road. Automatic gas pumps are also rare. The hose is usually equipped with a tap, and the customer fills the tank himself. When the attendant — almost always a woman — has set the desired number of gallons, 12 for example, then 12 gallons flow through the hose regardless of the tank's capacity. If there is no tap on the hose, the surplus simply runs into the ground. For this reason, service stations always reek of gas. I would often have appreciated some water to clean the windshield, but usually neither water nor a bucket was available.

5

4

We made good progress on the straight, well-paved roads and reached Kiev by nightfall. We drove to the Dniepro Hotel. While Oleg was trying to book a room for us — it was Saturday night — people crowded around the car again, examining it with great curiosity. Someone discovered that, because of the air springs, he could make the car "kneel" by touching it with one finger. Soon everyone was poking at the car. A few people even crawled underneath it, utterly fascinated by this technical miracle from beyond Russia's borders. Since I speak no Russian, I could only say *nyet* in response to all the questions. Oleg had managed to get the last double room. Prices for single and double rooms are virtually the same in the Soviet Union; there is a charge of just one ruble more for the second person.

Kiev, the capital of the Ukraine, is the third-largest city in Russia, with 1,632,000 inhabitants. This is where Oleg grew up. Since his mother and many friends live here, he spent half the night on the telephone in our room. Hotels do not charge for local calls, even if one talks for hours.

6 *At the market in Kiev.* It was very difficult to take pictures. Was it because people distrusted me as a foreigner, or were they generally suspicious? In any case, I learned to handle the camera as unobtrusively as possible. Occasionally Oleg had to put in a good word for me.

In a park where I wanted to photograph a child, I encountered hostility on the part of the young father pushing the carriage. Perhaps the people were so reserved because Oleg and I spoke German to each other. This would not have surprised me, considering the suffering caused by Hitler's invasion of the Ukraine. Four and a half million civilians were killed, more than 2 million were deported to Germany, and over 700 towns, 25,000 villages, and some 15,000 factories were destroyed in the Ukraine alone. And outside Kiev there is a ravine known as Babi Yar, where Hitler's special commandos shot over 75,000 Jews.

7 *Golden spires of St. Sophia Cathedral with the monument to Bogdan Khmelnitskiy in Kiev.* The interior of this church, now a museum, is richly decorated with eleventh-century frescoes. The cathedral is well frequented, and there is great interest in the church treasures.

Old Kiev is built on the heights above the Dnieper Valley. The view from here is considered among the most beautiful in the entire Soviet Union. A statue of Prince Vladimir, who introduced Christianity to the Ukraine, stands on the hillside. Beyond the river one can see the new housing and industry that are mushrooming around Kiev.

8 *Kiev beach on the Dnieper.* A new suspension bridge provides pedestrian access to the beach along the banks of the Dnieper below Kiev.

We drove on toward Moscow, a distance of some 560 miles, via Orel and Tula. Thanks to the quality of the road, we made good progress, but road signs were scarce. In larger cities Oleg had to ask the way several times before we could find the main route out again. Shortly before nightfall we reached Orel, where we spent the night at the local campground. Simple wooden cottages, each furnished with two bunks, a table, and chairs, were built into the trees. Campers are issued sheets and a towel when they register. Unfortunately, the sanitary conditions left much to be desired. Oleg warned me when he came back from the "john". I had no choice but to use the filthy, antediluvian facilities.

Moscow

Between Kiev and Moscow we left the Ukraine and entered the Russian Soviet Federated Socialist Republic—in other words, Russia proper—straddling two continents, stretching eastward to the Pacific Ocean and the Bering Straits; the Russia of immense steppes, the vast taiga, mighty rivers, active volcanoes, deserts and arctic ice; the Russia of endless tiny villages, numerous cities, and the great metropolis—Moscow!

9 *Kalinin Prospect in Moscow.* The route from Poland to Moscow via Minsk and Smolensk leads into the city along this boulevard. While Nikita Khrushchev was in power, he had this part of the city, one of Moscow's oldest, razed and rebuilt with modern housing and business sections. Housing developments in Russia are sometimes rather bleak, with their endless monotonous rows of six- to eight-story units. Along the Kalinin Prospect, however, vertical elements have been introduced to relieve the monotony of the horizontal. Prefabricated mass production has found far more widespread application in the Soviet Union than in countries of the West. It seems to me, though, that this spur to rapid development is concomitant with an oppressive uniformity.

A room was still available in Russia's largest hotel, the new Rossiya, centrally located directly opposite the Kremlin and the Cathedral of St. Basil. Oleg spent the night at home; he lives in a three-room flat in Moscow with his wife and two children. The Rossiya Hotel has 3,000 rooms and over 5,000 beds and caters to large congresses and major political meetings, a frequent occurrence in Moscow. The restaurants in the hotel are usually reserved for these visitors, and since I was not admitted to any of them, I retired on an empty stomach. The next day a receptionist showed me to a small restaurant on the second floor, which is always open to tourists. I had already wandered about this monstrous labyrinth of a hotel vainly searching for that very restaurant. Even my guide had trouble finding it. When we

finally got there, she apologized, saying she had been working at the Rossiya for only a month. The menu, printed in Russian, English, and German, offered a choice of twenty-five meat dishes. Actually one could order only chicken for 2 rubles, 92 kopeks (about $ 3.00), or shashlik for 1 ruble, 50 kopeks (about $ 1.50). On subsequent stays at the Rossiya I learned that that day was no exception. The choice was always the same: chicken or shashlik.

10 *Leo Tolstoy Street in Moscow.* This street, formerly called Dolga Khamovnichesky Lane, lies in a section of Moscow where many streets, untouched by modern building trends, have retained much of the charm and typical Russian atmosphere of Tolstoy's day. The rainwater from the gutters flows directly onto the streets and sidewalks. In spring the runoff from the snow on the roofs forms puddles at the bottom of the drainpipes; during cold nights these freeze, causing quite a hazard for pedestrians.

11 *Little girl in a kindergarten.* There are some 50,000 kindergartens and nursery schools for preschool children in the Russian Republic alone. The State also provides a wide range of services for mothers and children: maternity homes, consultation centers, children's clinics, children's hospitals, and convalescent homes.

On a previous trip to the U.S.S.R., I had arranged to be in Moscow for May Day. Red Square was already set up for the parade before the end of April. Red, white, and blue signs were painted on the ground to ensure maximum order and precision as the troops and hundreds of thousands of other participants paraded by. Opposite the Rossiya Hotel, vehicles decorated with posters and political slogans lined up ready to join the parade. The Historical Museum and the department store, Gum, were also festooned with enormous banners and pictures.
Although the parade did not begin until 10 A.M., Oleg and

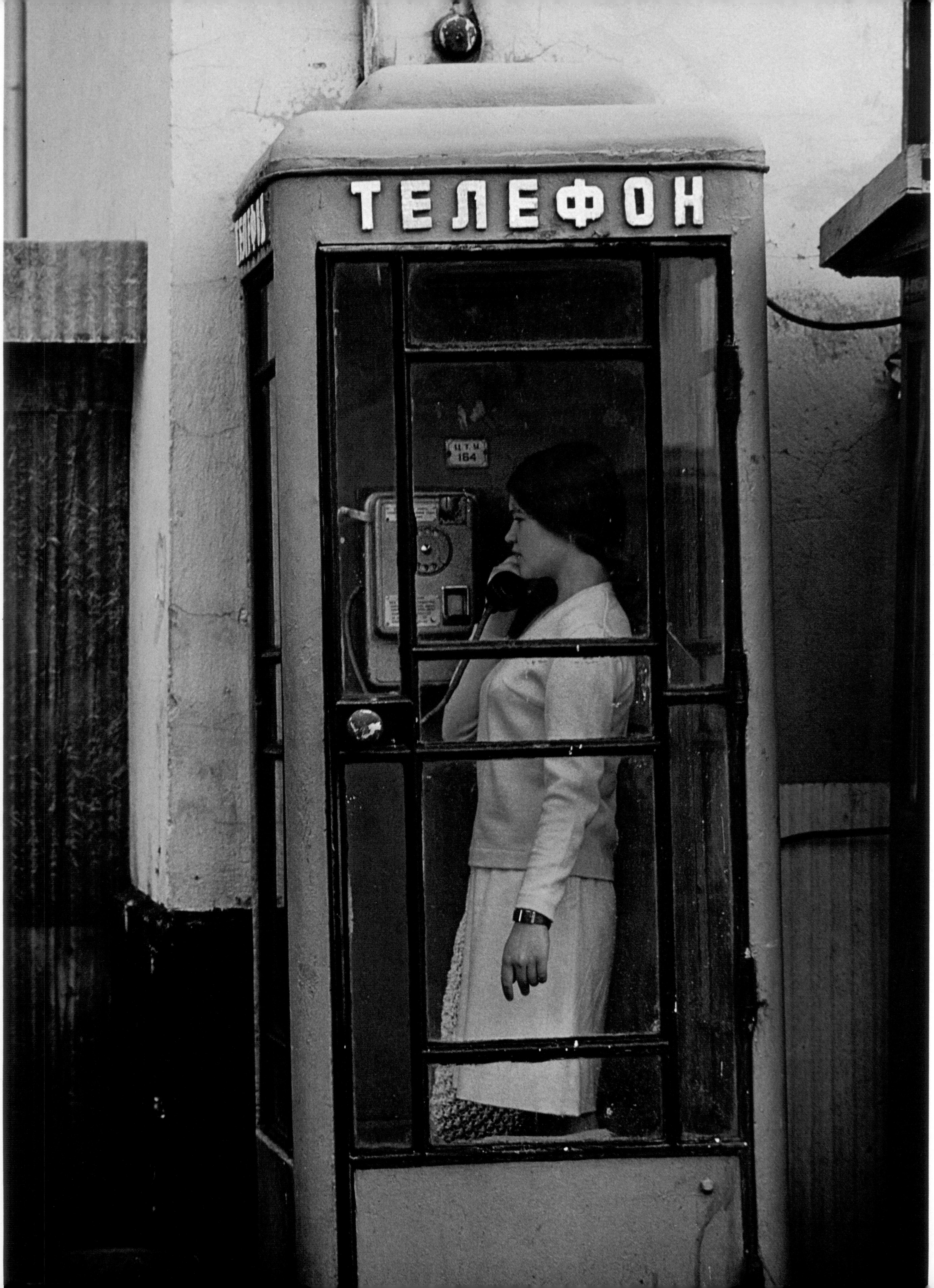
ТЕЛЕФОН

I—armed with food, drink, and photographic equipment—encamped on a projecting roof of the Cathedral of St. Basil, where a platform had been reserved for the press. On the way to the cathedral, which was directly opposite our hotel, we had to show our press passes eight times.

Foot soldiers of the army, navy, and air force lined up for the parade with admirable precision. Shortly before ten the chief dignitaries of the party, government, and army took their places on the balustrade of the Lenin Mausoleum. Interestingly, the fiftieth anniversary of the October Revolution was the last time that military troops participated in the May Day parade.

12   *May Day parade.*   The parade began as the clock on the Kremlin
13   tower struck ten. Military bands played, the cheers of the various military contingents resounded across the square, and the chief of the Red Army, Marshal Andrei A. Grechko, took the salute in an open car. Then all the detachments paraded past the Lenin Mausoleum. The motorized units approached the square from both sides of the Historical Museum—the smaller vehicles first, followed by regular tanks, armored tanks, and artillery. The square was filled with noise and with the stench of exhaust fumes hovering overhead in a bluish cloud. Intercontinental ballistic missiles brought up the rear in this impressive demonstration of military might, rolling by in eerie silence on their specially constructed carriages.

14   *May Day sports parade.*   The sports clubs came directly behind the last missile. They filled the entire width of the square and made a striking display in their colorful gym suits. The parade had clearly been organized with an eye to rhythmical effect. After the youth organizations, the Komsomols, had paraded past, there was an endless train of workers carrying thousands of red flags, banners, flowers, portraits of Lenin, and pictures of party and government heads. Five hours later the parade drew to a close.

I planned to use my own car for the trip south as well. We had to get special permits for such cities as Donetsk, Zhdanov, and Lugansk. Since the offices Oleg had to visit were scattered all over the city, I acted as chauffeur.

15   *Telephone booth in Moscow.*   Oleg used the telephone in my hotel room as much as possible, but occasionally we had to use a pay phone. It is understandable that we became a bit impatient when this young lady—charming as she might have been—occupied the booth for a lengthy chat.

Theoretically, telephone booths are equipped with directories, but I never saw one—anywhere. Everyone simply carries the numbers he needs in his own notebook.

Zagorsk — Kazan — Kharkov — Donetsk

Before traveling south, we made a side trip to Zagorsk, some one and a half hours by car to the north of Moscow. A second side trip took us to Kazan, which lies on the upper Volga two hours by air from Moscow.

16 *Zagorsk, the last place of pilgrimage in the Soviet Union.* Zagorsk was once one of the holiest cities in Russia; even the tsars had to approach it on foot. Today it is still a place of pilgrimage, harboring one of Russia's three remaining seminaries, and is therefore an important center of the Russian Orthodox Church. Once inside the walls, the visitor looks upon an entire city of golden and multicolored domes, churches, bell towers, fountains, and monastery buildings. Old peasant women are virtually the only ones who make this pilgrimage nowadays. They sit huddled on steps here and there with their bundles resting beside them. The sacred quarter is situated on a hill.

17 *Service in the Church of the Trinity at Zagorsk.* Sunlight streams through the windows into an interior rich in gold, icons, and frescoes. The people worship crowded together in the mystical semidarkness. The deacon sings the ancient litany of the Orthodox Church in a deep bass voice which alternates with the monks' choir. The women huddle still closer together, sobbing or weeping aloud.

"Mother Volga", the principal waterway of the western U.S.S.R., is celebrated in many Russian songs. The river is some 2,300 miles long and empties into the Caspian Sea. There are several important industrial centers in the valley of the Volga such as Gorkiy, formerly known as Nizhni Novgorod; Kazan, the capital of the Tatar Republic; Kuybyshev, the ninth-largest city in the Soviet Union; Volgograd, formerly Stalingrad; and Astrakhan at the mouth of the river.

18 *Kazan, a river station on the Volga.* Three-tiered passenger steamers ply the river between Gorkiy and Astrakhan. Although the three- to four-day journey through the plains tends to be monotonous, there is a great deal of lively activity at the river stations.

The Volga has been the site of many of the most important events in the history of Russia: Tsar Ivan IV, the Terrible, conquered the Tatar states in 1552; here the cossack rebel, Stenka Razin, hero of numerous ballads, fought against tsar and landowner in the seventeenth century. In 1918 the fate of the Soviet Union hung in the balance when the counterrevolutionary White Army besieged the territory held by the Red Army in Tsaritsyn, later called Stalingrad and known as Volgograd today. Stalin, who had been authorized by the Communist Party to stop here and organize food supplies for Moscow, immediately recognized the gravity of the situation, took the command into his own hands, and won the decisive battle for the revolution. Twenty-three years later the Volga was a focal point of world history once again, when the German army under Field Marshal Friedrich Paulus suffered an annihilating defeat here.

19 *House in Kazan where Lenin lived as a young man.* Vladimir Ilyich Ulyanov was born in Simbirsk, now called Ulyanovsk, of a well-to-do Russian family. Later he moved to Kazan with his mother to study law at the university there. Lenin lived in this house, now a popular museum, from 1887 to 1889. It was here that he was arrested for participating in a demonstration against the head of the university.

We made the final preparations to head south from Moscow. The day before we were scheduled to leave, I discovered that during the night both halogen fog lamps and the backup lights had been taken off my car and that the side mirror had been

23

22

wrenched off. Oleg, who was almost more annoyed than I, went to the police. There he was told that a Russian car had been worked over in our area the same night and in this case the thieves had made off with the four wheels as well. One can often read about such thefts in Russian newspapers; this "organizing" of spare automobile parts is widespread, since the parts fetch stupendous prices on the black market.

The drive to Kursk, some 300 miles south of Moscow, went smoothly. However, the Western motorist must always be on the alert for surprises: a harvester suddenly crosses the street, road construction signs are nonexistent or, at best, appear much too late to do any good, objects that have fallen off trucks or farm machines are left lying in the middle of the road. On the outskirts of Kursk I saw a jagged chunk of iron too late to swerve out of the way and demolished the muffler and exhaust pipe as a result. Making a deafening racket, we drove through the evening traffic in Kursk, looking for a garage, but they were all closed for the night. While looking for accommodations along a main thoroughfare, I pulled out to pass a bus stop and found myself on the tram line, the rails of which were sunk almost a foot and a half into the street. My car ended up suspended on its chassis. I glanced quickly into the rearview mirror and just had time to shout at Oleg, "Watch out!", when a tram crashed into us, denting the whole left side of the car up to the windshield. Oleg got out. Of course, a huge crowd gathered. A policeman surveyed the situation, gestured to the crowd, and in no time flat a dozen people grabbed hold of the car and lifted it out of the ditch with me still behind the steering wheel. At first I was afraid our journey had come to an end, but soon we found that only the body of the car had been damaged. We simply adjusted to the fact that the doors on the left were permanently closed.

20 *Kharkov, second-largest city in the Ukraine.* Compared to Kiev, Kharkov is a young city, hardly more than 300 years old. A tractor plant, the second largest in the Soviet Union, was erected here in 1931, and prior to the war almost a quarter of a million tractors had already come off the production line.

Outside Kharkov we turned off the "tourist route" and drove into the "closed district", the Donets Basin, a center of heavy industry, especially coal mining and steel production. Special permits are required to visit such cities as Donetsk, Zhdanov, and Lugansk, and a policeman whistled us down from his glass cabin. An official sternly examined our permits and my visa. We were allowed to drive on.

21 *Change of shift at the October Coal Mine in Donetsk.* A few miners
22 accompanied us into the October mine. We rode for about a mile on the tram road at a depth of 1,300 feet, then stooped through an adit to reach one of the bores. Unfortunately, I could not take any pictures because I was not allowed to use flash equipment.

23 *Radio control center at the October mine in Donetsk.* The mine with its modern hoist is quite impressive. It is not surprising that record hauls of coal are frequent here.

24 *Industrial landscape, Donetsk.* In addition to Donetsk, there are hundreds of other smaller and larger industrial cities in the Donets Basin. The district is immensely rich in coal, which is said to amount to some 135 billion tons.

Zhdanov — Lugansk — Rostov-on-the-Don — Baku

The following serves to illustrate that we were in a region closed to Western tourists. When we went to return the key to our hotel room, the chambermaid, who was responsible for keys to all the rooms in the hotel, asked us to wait at the door until she had inspected the room. This seems to be standard practice in hotels for Soviet citizens. The chambermaid has to make sure that the mirror is still in one piece and that no towels or the like are missing.

We drove past vast corn fields on an excellent new road and reached Zhdanov — 75 miles away — in less than an hour and a half. Zhdanov is the principal port on the north shore of the Sea of Azov, which is connected to the Black Sea by the narrow Kerch Straits.

25 *Asovstal Metallurgical Works in Zhdanov.* The industrialization of the Donets Basin began a century ago when John Hughs, an English entrepreneur, built the first smelting works on the shores of the Kalmius River in 1869. Today smokestacks, blast furnaces, and elevators are characteristic of the industrialized Ukraine.

26 *Open-hearth furnaces at the Asovstal Metallurgical Works in Zhdanov.* A foreman accompanied us on a tour over soot-covered grounds to the various sections of the rambling works. Our last stop was the large bay which houses the impressive open-hearth furnaces. The Ukraine, I was told, produces 10 percent of the world's pig iron and 8 percent of the world's steel.

27 *Retired employees from the Zhdanov iron and steel works.* These men meet to pass the time near their former place of work. The signs at the entrance forbid smoking and driving through the plant.

28 *Streets of Lugansk.* The curiosity that our car provoked began to plague us. And the accident did not help matters. Cars in such

condition are not allowed on the road in the Soviet Union. As a result, the police kept stopping us; each time Oleg had to explain what had happened before we could go on. Whenever we drove into a city, I immediately headed for the side streets to avoid attracting attention.

29 *Diesel locomotive factory, October Revolution, Lugansk.* A number of locomotives under construction stand on rails in an enormous bay 2,890 feet long. According to a press release, Lugansk is to be called Voroshilovgrad again. This had been the name of the city from 1935 to 1958, in honor of a Ukrainian railroad employee's son who once worked in the locomotive factory. Kliment E. Voroshilov had a remarkable military career and became a marshal but fell into disgrace in 1958.

Before proceeding to Rostov-on-the-Don, 125 miles away, we visited the memorial to the soldiers who had fallen during World War II. Situated on a rise at the edge of the city, the memorial affords a magnificent view, including the battle-field between Lugansk and Stalingrad where Field Marshal Paulus's army was trapped.

30 *View upstream at Rostov-on-the-Don.* At 4:30 A.M. we drove to the large bridge over the Don, which I had explored the previous evening to find a good location for shooting the sunrise. I did not realize that two policemen were watching me as I drove across the security line to take a shortcut to the parking lot at the head of the bridge. They approached us smiling — not a word about the security line. It was the car they were interested in, especially the engine. Rostov is a city for tourists. One can take pictures anywhere, even from this bridge, which is unusual. "But only upstream," the policemen kindly called to us, "not downstream. Downstream it's forbidden."

28

27

36

35

31 *Fishermen's walk on the Don in Rostov.*

32 *In the assembly bay at the Agricultural Machine Plant No. 1 in Rostov-*
33 *on-the-Don.* The various parts of the harvesting machines — bodies, engines, wheels — move in on rails from all sides to the conveyor belt where the final assembly of the harvesters takes place. A finished colossus leaves the bay every three and a half minutes and is transported by tractor to a lot where hundreds of machines are already waiting to be shipped out.

Since we wanted to make a side trip to Baku by air, we left the car at the hotel parking lot, which is guarded around the clock. The 620-mile flight took less than two and a half hours.

34 *Oil fields in Baku.* We hired a taxi for our first tour. The driver, called Napoleon, took us directly to the oldest oil fields, pictures of which are rarely found in official publications. Unforgettable is the impression of sights and sounds made by the forest of rusty iron filled with the groaning, whistling, and wheezing of the slowly moving pumps.

35 *View of Baku from the Kirov Memorial.* Baku, the city of black gold, is the capital of the Azerbaijan S.S.R. With a population of 1,261,000, it is the fifth-largest city in the Soviet Union. The city spreads out like an amphitheater along a bluff of the Apsheron Peninsula on the Caspian Sea. Baku, which has been so called since the seventh century, was a city of great importance in the Middle Ages; in fact, as early as the days of the Greeks, oil had been found here. Many palaces and mosques in the city hark back to three centuries of Persian supremacy. An important cultural center, Baku boasts a university, the Academy of Sciences, several technological institutes, theaters, and concert halls.
Industrial exploitation of the immensely rich petroleum resources began in the mid-nineteenth century. The Swedish industrialists

Robert and Ludwig Nobel, brothers of Nobel Prize founder Alfred, and an interest by the House of Rothschild were instrumental in unlocking the riches, stimulating the export of Russian petroleum, and helping to develop an efficient distribution network throughout the country. At the beginning of this century Sir Henry Deterding, head of the Royal Dutch Shell Company, gave further impetus to the Russian oil industry.

36 *The Mausoleum of the Twenty-six Commissars from Baku.* The twenty-six commissars formed the first Soviet government in Baku. In 1919, at the peak of the Russian Revolution, English troops intervened in the city and had the commissars captured, kidnapped, and executed. Only one escaped, concealed in a coal sack and loaded onto a ship by longshoremen. He was Anastas Ivanovich Mikoyan, a Baku native of Armenian origin, who has since played a major role in the Communist Party and was one of the top leaders in the Kremlin for more than thirty years.

The return flight to Rostov was breathtaking. As the plane rose above the cloud bank, all the mountains of the Caucasus range spread out before us. I could clearly discern the two peaks of Mount Elbrus.

On the way from Rostov to the Caucasus, we reentered the territory of the Russian Republic and drove on excellent roads through the plains of the Kuban District, the black earth region. The freshly plowed fields covered with a fine veil of green extended all the way to the horizon. We stopped at a gas station. There was no high-test pump, but the attendant sold us his last 20-liter container at a slightly higher price. We then turned off the main road and drove into the mountains to the Kurort Teberda. *Kurort*, the German word for "resort", has been integrated into the Russian language. (Russian has also borrowed other German, French, and English words such as *Buchhalter* (bookkeeper), *Kapital*, *Schlagbaum* (railway barrier), *étage* (floor), *toilette*, pullover, telephone, and interview.) The Motorists' Pension, recommended by the gas station attendant, turned out to be a disappointment. Service in the dining room was less than friendly, the beds were poor, and the sagging wire-mesh mattresses tortured my back.

Early in the morning we drove to Dombay, nestled in the far corner of the valley. There we climbed a small hill to get a view of the autumn mountains. On the way back we turned into the Klukhor Valley, which we had discovered on the map. Although the road was not very steep, the car had great difficulty climbing. The "high test" that we had bought for such a fancy price turned out to be the lowest octane gas.

37 *Mountains around the Klukhorsky Pass in the Caucasus.* We learned from the map that Khakel, the peak in the middle, has an altitude of 11,950 feet and that Buulgen, the one on the right, an altitude of 12,840 feet. The road over the Klukhorsky Pass, when completed, will be the shortest route between the northern Caucasus and Sukhumi on the Black Sea.

38 *Shepherd with typical fur cap.* We encountered several large flocks of sheep, the major source of income for the people of the Caucasus. Cattle-raising has recently been introduced into this region.

39 *Georgian military highway in the Caucasus.* The Georgian military highway, the most interesting part of the Caucasian tour, begins after Ordzhonikidze. The ruins of the legendary fortress of Queen Tamara, great granddaughter of King David the Restorer, stand in the Devil's Gorge, the narrowest point of the Terek. This narrow gorge, an ideal spot for pirates and highway robbers, once marked the doom of many a traveler and caravan. In 1829, Alexander Pushkin only risked the journey in the company of a cossack escort and a cannon. Today an excellent road leads through the gorge and up the valley over screes and past ruins and watchtowers perched here and there on promontories jutting out overhead.

40 *"Glory to the Great Stalin".* While driving along the Georgian military highway, we passed these words painted in big white letters on a retaining wall. Stalin, the fourth child of the cobbler Vissarion Dzhugashvili, was born December 21, 1879, not far from here in the heart of Georgia. He is still greatly admired by his fellow countrymen. The name Stalin has lost none of its fascination for the thousands who annually visit his birthplace in Gori.

41 *Kazbegi, a mountain village in the Caucasus.* The Georgian military highway passes through small, picturesque villages and former caravanserais. We bought locally grown grapes and tomatoes. Mount Kazbek, the highest peak in the southern Caucasus (16,560 feet), rises above the fog which has enveloped its snowcapped neighbors.
The higher we climbed, the more brilliant were the autumn colors. The highest point of the pass was shrouded in fog. A sign read 2,395 meters (7,859 feet) above sea level. It was very cold at this altitude. Occasionally the fog lifted just enough to permit a

42

43

glimpse of extensive alpine pastures with large flocks of grazing sheep. A good road with hairpin curves and long straight stretches took us down into the valley, and we approached Tbilisi, formerly known as Tiflis, the capital of Georgia.

We arrived in Tbilisi before dark, time enough to drive up David's Mountain, named after King David, who made Georgia one of the most powerful states in the Near East during the eleventh and twelfth centuries. The winding, well-paved mountain road leads through a forest of cypress trees to the summit, which falls off steeply on one side. This spot affords a magnificent view of the city and the meandering Kura River valley, along which old Tiflis spreads out, revealing its ancient Georgian structures, its churches, mosques, and fortresses.

42 *Modern buildings in Tbilisi.*

In Tbilisi I expected a letter from my wife. At general delivery in the post office, I showed my passport, and the girl looked through a fat bundle of letters — rather cursorily, it seemed to me. *Nyet…* nothing. I told Oleg this was impossible. He asked the girl to look again. Annoyed at my questioning her veracity, she glared at me and repeated that there was no letter for me. It was my turn to be annoyed. In good Swiss German I reiterated that I was quite certain there was one. With a withering glance at the obstinate foreigner, she finally checked the bundle again. Sure enough, it was there. Without another word she handed me the letter.
I decided to cut our travel plans short, since I had been fighting a stubborn sinus infection for days. Oleg tried to telephone Novorossiysk to move up our reservations on the ferry to Yalta. Neither his call nor my call to Switzerland went through.

We drove on 140 miles without finding a service station that sold high-test gas, and finally I was forced to use my emergency supply, a 20-liter container that I had brought along from Switzerland. We just made it to Kutaisi, where I bought gas and re-filled my container.
The road between Kutaisi and Okhamkhire to the Black Sea was poor. Deep holes and gashes in the asphalt were unmarked, and there were never any signs at the intersections. We did not reach Okhamkhire until well after dark and had to share a room with someone because the hotel was filled. Our neighbor was already in bed and turned his face to the wall when we came in. After sleeping for only a short time, I awoke to the sound of unbelievably loud snoring. Oleg woke up, too. Just two days before, under similar circumstances, Oleg had told me about an old cure for snoring. One simply chirps into the ear of the person in question. To my astonishment Oleg actually crawled out of bed, approached our snoring Georgian, and chirped into his ear four or five times without success. In spite of my valiant efforts to the contrary I simply could not help laughing. The comrade awakened and sleepily asked what on earth was going on.

43 *At the beach in Sochi on the Black Sea.*   Although it was late in the season, early October, the beach here was full of life in comparison to others on the Black Sea. On the narrow, rocky strip along the promenade crowds of people lay basking in the sun.

Black Sea Coast — Yalta — Odessa — Kishinev

At Sochi, back in the Russian Republic again, we tried to telephone Novorossiysk, but after waiting for several hours, we had to give up. We were told, as before, that the cable was probably damaged. We sent a telegram. The weather, which had been good so far, took a turn for the worse. The much-praised Black Sea coast did not appeal to me. Perhaps it was the rain, perhaps the pain and discomfort from my sinusitis.

44 *Coastline on the Black Sea between Tuapse and Novorossiysk.* The hard and soft layers of the Caucasian folds are very beautiful here. Shallow water along the coast reveals the eroded shelf underneath the waves.

At the harbor in Novorossiysk we learned that the ferry to Yalta on the Crimean Peninsula would not sail for two days. While Oleg was looking for an alternative, I saw the *Grusia*, a cruise liner scheduled to sail for Yalta at 6 P.M. I asked Oleg to inquire if we might not get passage on this ship. First we were told that they were booked up, then that our vehicle could not be loaded aboard because the crane was unsafe. Finally, after I signed a waiver for damages should the winch fail, the car was heaved aboard and safely stowed away in the hold. The boat sailed just eight minutes late. The captain, Anatoli Garagula, had told us that the cabins were unfortunately all taken and that we would have to fend for ourselves as best we could. When the ship had sailed out of the harbor, Oleg and I sought out the captain on the bridge to thank him. He gave us a good-natured smile and told us that a first-class cabin was available after all, as an important official had disembarked at Novorossiysk.

After taking a shower and changing into fresh shirts, we visited the captain again and gave him the last copy I had of my Africa book, with a dedication from both of us. He invited us for a glass of cognac. He confirmed that he had originally rejected our request, passed on to him by the first mate. However, when Oleg

had approached him personally and had told him so many good things about the foreigner in his company, he had changed his mind. Now he was happy to have made our acquaintance and invited us to join him for dinner.

The captain spoke English quite well. He asked me to describe some of my experiences and wanted to know if I had met ships' captains from other countries. I told him about Commander Price Lewis, captain of the U.S. Navy icebreaker U.S.S. *Staten Island*, whom I had joined on lengthy voyages in the Antarctic. We drank a toast to the pleasure of meeting friendly, interesting people all over the world.

Before sunrise the next morning I went on deck. We were already quite close to Yalta, and the broad tip of the peninsula was bathed in the exquisite light of the rising sun. The *Grusia* docked in Yalta at exactly 8 A.M. We went to take leave of the captain, but instead he invited us to remain on board for breakfast. And what a breakfast! Cheese, sausage, salad, shashlik — more tender than I had ever eaten before — and cognac. We also consumed, for the first and last time, a considerable amount of alcohol for breakfast. Once more we exchanged warm farewells, and the captain cordially invited us to be his guests again. He accompanied us to my car, which was still on board, as I had asked the first mate to notify me before unloading it. My car? I hardly recognized it. There it stood washed sparkling clean.

In Yalta, Oleg took me to a hospital where a woman physician examined me. I was worried about my sinuses; the pain was almost unbearable. Oleg knew that under no circumstances did I wish to be hospitalized. Were there no alternative, I intended to go straight back to Switzerland. There was not much the doctor could do; she prescribed Pyramidon, which I had already purchased at a pharmacy in Murmansk. This seems to be a cure-all in the U.S.S.R. for it had also been prescribed for me by a

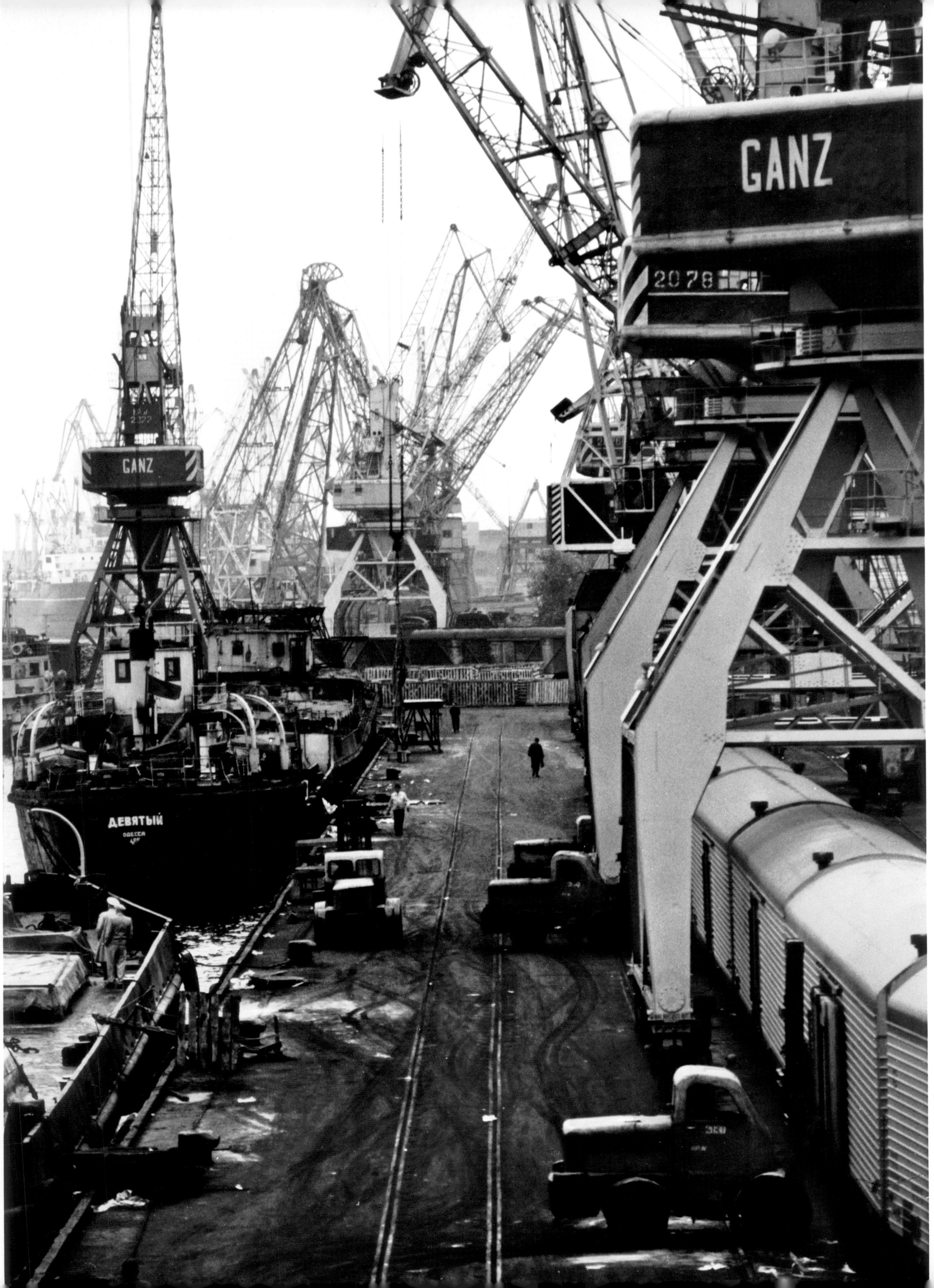
GANZ
2078
GANZ
ДЕВЯТЫЙ
ОДЕССА

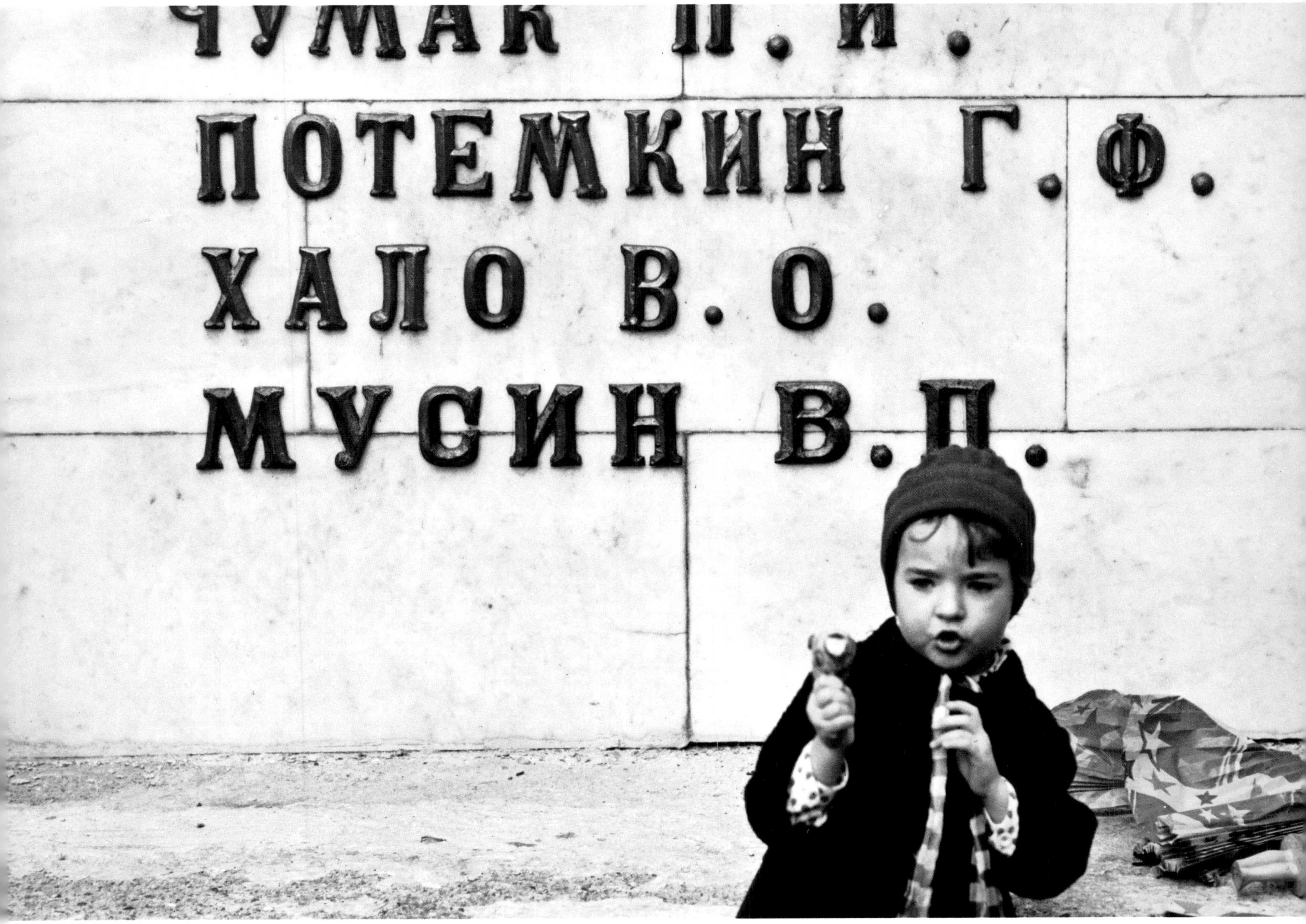
ЧУМАК П. И.
ПОТЕМКИН Г. Ф.
ХАЛО В. О.
МУСИН В. П.

doctor in Moscow when I twisted my ankle on the steps of the Hotel Metropol.

In Yalta the police stopped us again. This time we were told we could not drive on until the car had been repaired. The officials demanded proof from the Kursk police that a streetcar had really rammed into us. We suggested that they themselves telephone the police in Kursk for confirmation.

After Simferopol we drove through nothing but vineyards for more than 60 miles. This is the home of the famous Crimean wine, well-known even beyond Russia's borders. Soon we were passing through the endless Ukrainian plains again, through vast newly plowed fields of rich black earth. We turned off the main road and drove to Askaniya Nova, a wildlife reservation in the steppes where a herd of Prshobalsky wild horses, the Siberian ibex, deer, a small herd of bison, and other species are protected in vast game preserves.

In Kherson we crossed the lower Dnieper and reached Odessa in two hours. We drove to the center of the city along the Deribazovskaya, the main thoroughfare, and took a room in the Kraznaya Hotel. Odessa, founded in 1794 and now one of the biggest cities in the Ukraine, has a surprising variety of architectural styles dating back well into prerevolutionary Russia.

45 *Port of Odessa.* Odessa is the most important Ukrainian port on the Black Sea and home base for the two whaling fleets the Slava and the Sovietskaya Ukraina. The recently completed passenger terminal stands next to the modern dockyards with their tangle of cranes.

46 *Memorial stone to the heroes of the revolution in Odessa.*

47 *"Potemkin Stairs" in Odessa.* A statue of Duc de Richelieu, governor-general in 1803, stands in the middle of the round "square" on Primorskiy Boulevard, from which a flight of stairs with 192 steps and ten landings leads directly down to the harbor. Here the Russian film director Sergei Mikhailovich Eisenstein shot some of the most famous scenes from his film *Potemkin*, which depicts the 1905 mutiny of the crew of the battleship *Potemkin*, in sympathy with a general strike in Odessa. Before long the *Potemkin* came to be regarded as a symbol of the revolution.

I tried to ring Zurich from the hotel. After waiting for two hours, I was informed that the call could not go through because the cable was out of order. Apparently the telephone system does not function over long distances. However, we were disturbed by local calls half the night. Oleg explained that, as in other cities, the calls came from women looking for "work".

We drove along hilly roads through the Moldavian Republic via the capital, Kishinev, to Leusheny on the Russian-Rumanian border. Here our ways parted. Oleg took the train back to Moscow; I drove home by way of Rumania, Yugoslavia, and Italy.

Murmansk — Leningrad

I returned to the Soviet Union upon receiving a telegram from the Swiss Embassy in Moscow informing me that I would be allowed to join a marine expedition in the north. When I arrived in Moscow, the Soviet authorities knew nothing about this offer, and I was told, furthermore, that the official responsible in this matter was out of town. In any event, I decided to go up to Murmansk and Leningrad. Perhaps upon my return someone would know whether the expedition to Dickson on the Arctic Ocean, to Haze Island, and to Franz Josef Land was going to take place.

In an overcrowded train I traveled almost seven and a half hours to Leningrad; then on to Murmansk, another twenty-six hours. The train crossed the Arctic Circle near the coast of the White Sea about 180 miles south of Murmansk. During the trip I managed to talk with a good many people, mostly in English. The conductor, a woman, found a seat for me in the crowded dining car and helped me order something to eat. Life in the train: chance meetings, a placid *babushka*, crying children, men playing chess, people eating out of bags and baskets. Someone even offered me a swig from the vodka bottle that was being passed around.

48 *Little Ivan in Murmansk.* Here the stereotyped Western notion of people dressed in plain and shabby clothes is given the lie. Quite the contrary proved to be the case, especially in the Arctic Zone. The children's clothing is practical and well made. After only four years in the north, workers receive a special allowance amounting to 120 percent of the basic wage. There are miners and fishermen in Murmansk who earn as much as 1,000 rubles a month (more than $ 1,000), depending on their diligence and the length of their stay.

49 *Lenin Prospect in Murmansk.* Murmansk, situated on the Kola

Peninsula, was founded in 1916 and today has a population of some 300,000.

50 *View of the harbor in Murmansk.* Since it is free of ice all year, Murmansk is the principal port in the Arctic Zone for Russian seaborne traffic across the Atlantic. During the forty-month siege of Murmansk in World War II, 70 percent of the city and the harbor was destroyed. Today Murmansk is the most important fishing port in the Soviet Union. The extensive harbor, with its shipyards, metal factories, and fish-processing plants, is also the home port of the first atomic-powered icebreaker in the world, the *Lenin*.

With a journalist and the director of the port I visited the "floating" fish factory, the *Sergei Vassilizin*. The twenty-eight-year-old captain showed us around the new Polish-made ship, which was to make its third voyage in a few days with a crew of 258 to join the herring fleet off the west coast of Norway.

51 *Leningrad.* This city of 100 islands and countless bridges on the Gulf of Finland was called St. Petersburg in tsarist Russia. Under the rule of Peter the Great in the early seventeenth century, the elite of Russia began building the new metropolis in the Neva Delta according to a bold and generous conception of city planning. This perfect model of a homogeneous, artistically unified architecture has retained its unique character throughout the varying currents of the centuries. The city, named Petrograd in 1914 and renamed Leningrad in 1924, the year of Lenin's death, witnessed the birth of the Soviet Union in 1917. The misery of the people finally erupted into what is known today as the February Revolution, and the Petrograd Soviet of Workers' and Soldiers' Deputies was established. On March 2 (March 15 by the Gregorian calendar, which Russia did not adopt until February 1, 1918) a committee of the Duma, the parliament, formed a pro-

52

53

visional government and took over the affairs of state. Nicholas II abdicated in favor of his brother Mikhail, who in turn renounced the throne on March 3, just one day later. Russia thus became a republic.

The October Revolution began October 25, 1917, according to the Julian calendar (November 7 according to the Gregorian calendar). The Second All-Russian Congress of Soviets convened in Petrograd a few days after the Bolsheviks had taken over the provisional government headed by Alexander Kerensky, which they replaced with the Military Revolutionary Committee. On October 24 (November 6) Bolshevik troops and the Workers' Militia under the command of Leon Trotsky occupied all the key points of the city with the exception of the Winter Palace, where the provisional government was housed, as they feared that it was too heavily guarded. The "ten days that shook the world" ran their course. When the Winter Palace was finally stormed on November 7, the revolutionaries suffered six casualties, the total losses of the October Revolution in Petrograd. The ministers still in the city were arrested; Kerensky escaped. Trotsky distributed a flier "to the citizens of Russia" in which he proclaimed that the provisional government had toppled; that the power now lay in the hands of the Petrograd Congress of Workers' and Soldiers' Deputies and the Military Revolutionary Committee; that a peace treaty was in preparation; that private property was to be abolished; and that workers were to be given control of production. In protest against the methods of the Bolsheviks the right-wing Social Revolutionaries and the Mensheviks, the moderate wing of the Social Democrats, withdrew from the Soviet Congress, thus paving the way for Lenin's rise to power. He soon became chairman of the Council of People's Commissars and the revolution began to take hold throughout the nation.

52 *Gun barrel of the cruiser* Aurora.   A shot in the air fired from this cannon at 9:40 P.M. on October 25 (November 7), 1917, was the signal to storm the Winter Palace. The crew of the cruiser had been won over by the Military Revolutionary Committee.

53 *Ice hole in the Neva.*   A large rectangle had been sawed out of the frozen river. A woman of about sixty proceeded barefoot down the steps hewn into the ice and took a leisurely swim in the "pool".

54 *Visitors at the Hermitage in Leningrad.*   Thousands of visitors from all over the world pass through these rooms daily. Here Russian girls are looking at two paintings by Pierre Auguste Renoir: *Child with Whip*, dated 1885, on the left and *Study of a Woman's Head*, probably 1875/1876, on the right.

55 *View from the Hermitage of the northeast corner of the Palace Square.* Russia's largest and most valuable collection of art, once the pride of Catherine II, is housed in a wing of the Winter Palace. This priceless collection of art treasures from ancient statues to French impressionists has grown over the centuries.

Art, architecture, broad boulevards, beautiful parks—all this is Leningrad. But no less important elements in the city are the machine factories, shipyards, and one of the largest ports in the Soviet Union. Aleksandr Solzhenitsyn tells how the Soviet people feel about this city: "So alien to us—and yet our greatest pride—this display of splendor. How magnificent it is to stroll along these avenues! But other Russians have had to grit their teeth; cursing, they perished in fog and morass in order to create all this splendor. It is a staggering thought that perhaps one day our own formless, wretched existence ... the groans of those put to death, the sobbing of their wives could also be forgotten. Will this, too, lead to perfect, immortal beauty?"

Moscow in Winter

Moscow is especially beautiful when the bulbous domes of the Kremlin are crowned with snow, and the people, muffled against the cold, stamp along in heavy boots. The city is picturesque not only on the few sunny days in winter, but even throughout the gray ice-cold months which one can endure only with great energy and forbearance.

56 *"Tsar-Pushka" cannon in the Kremlin.* The king of cannons cast by Master Chokhov in 1586 stands next to the Bell Tower of Ivan the Great. This monster weighs some 40 tons and boasts an 890-millimeter bore—nearly 3 feet!

57 *Vostok rocket in Moscow.* In the north of the city next to Ostankino Park is a huge site with more than 300 halls and pavilions in which the scientific and technical achievements of the Soviet Union are on exhibit. Especially popular is a life-size model of the Vostok rocket with which cosmonauts and spaceships are launched. At the bottom of the photograph one can just see the top of the new television tower, 1,650 feet high.

Moscow is a city of working people; over half of its 6 million inhabitants are employed. More than 120 machine factories lie within the city limits, which also contain one of the country's oldest food-processing centers. Moscow is the hub of the nation's railroads, and four airports daily serve tens of thousands of passengers headed for destinations all over the globe.

58 *View from the west side of Hotel Rossiya in Moscow.* From the twelfth floor of the hotel one has a magnificent view of the city: the Moskva, the Kremlin walls with imposing towers at the corners, and the vast sea of buildings in the center. A room here costs 19 rubles, more than $ 20. Nor is the price of a good breakfast—$ 1.50—by any means moderate.

59 *Volleyball game between the Red Army and Kharkov teams.* Shortly before the start of the game there was a burst of applause, and every head turned toward the grandstand where a man and a woman, both in officers' uniforms, had just taken their seats. From Shenya, my interpreter, I learned that they were Pavel Popovich, the fourth cosmonaut launched into space, and his wife.

60 *Changing of the guard in front of the Lenin Mausoleum on Red Square.* Three minutes before every hour, three soldiers, the Lenin Guard, appear in the gate of the Spasskaya Tower and march in parade step, guns shouldered, to the entrance of the Lenin Mausoleum. The changing of the guard runs with perfect precision, timed to begin with the first chime of the bells in the Spasskaya Tower. And, of course, there is always a crowd of spectators to watch the ceremony. Red Square is so named not out of any ideological considerations; in fact, the term goes back to the sixteenth century. The Russian word *krazny* means both "red" and "beautiful".

61 *Southeast corner of the Kremlin walls with the Moskvoretskaya Tower.* The Kremlin is enclosed by a triangular wall with nineteen towers of varying sizes. On the left, the road along the Moskva; on the right in the background, St. Basil's Cathedral; and behind it, Red Square. Inside the Kremlin walls, visible in delicate silhouette, the Bell Tower of Ivan the Great on the left and the buildings of the Presidium of the Supreme Soviet and the Kremlin Theater on the right.

62 *Troika race in the Moscow Hippodrome.* Oleg had no trouble getting me through the barriers onto the racetrack. A horse-lover and racing fan, he knew all the right people here. Races are held every Sunday. The troika races are by far the most popular. The excitement is great because bets can be placed and it is possible to win back the stakes several times over.

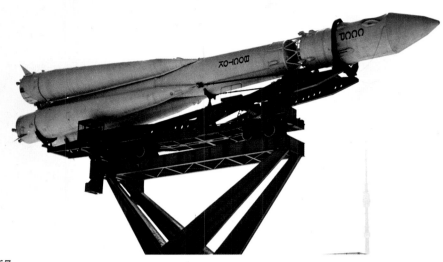

57

56

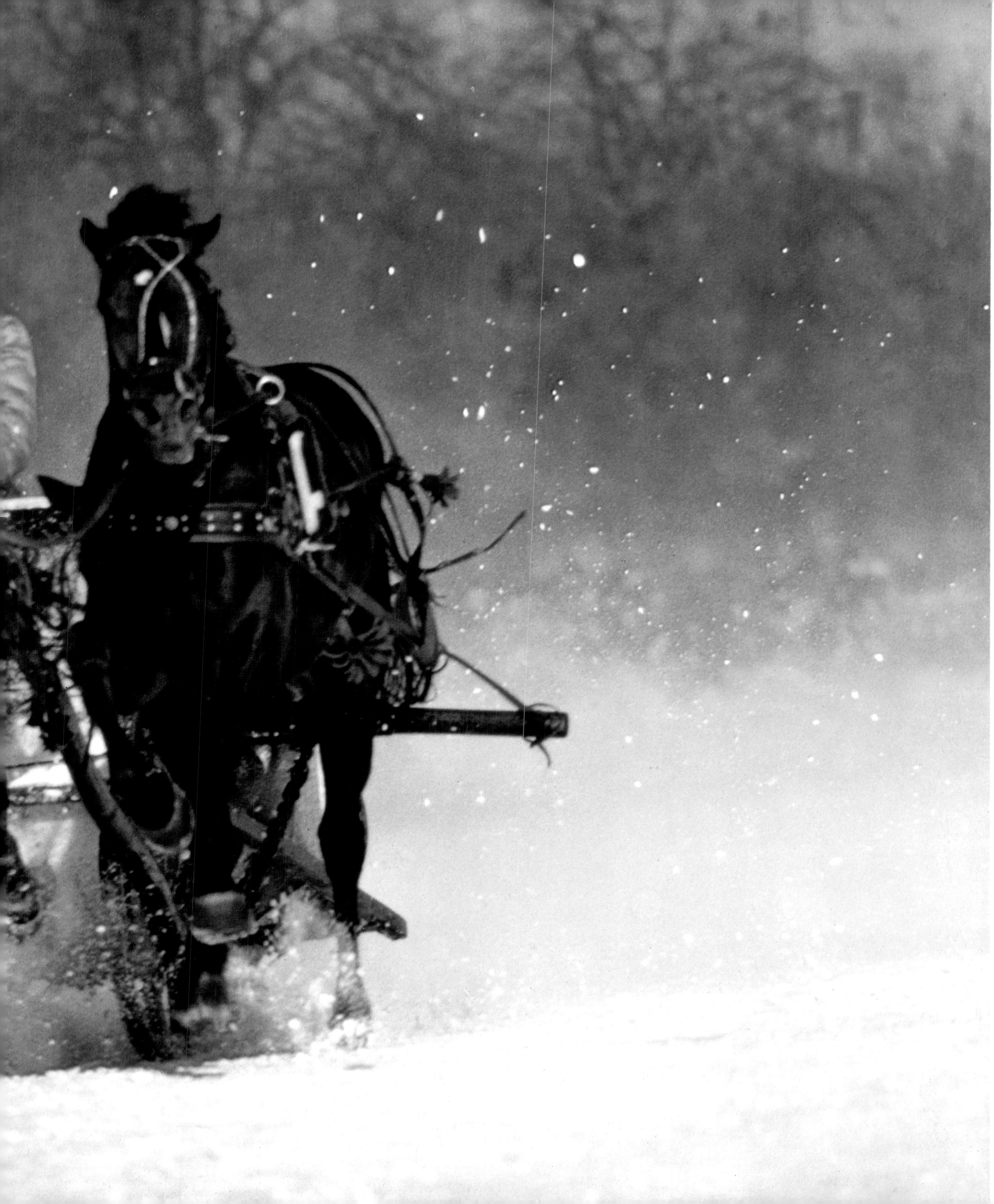

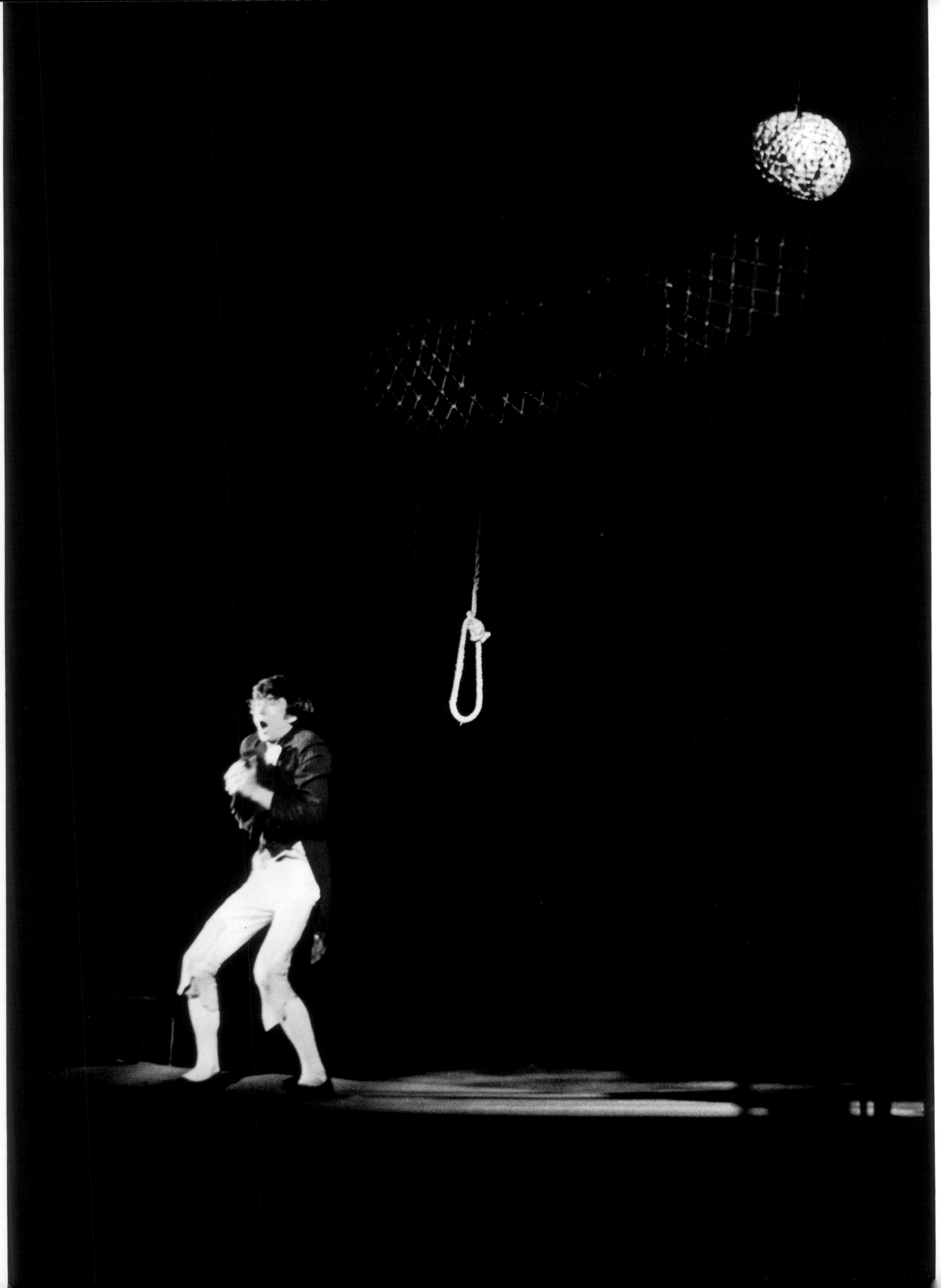

Moscow offers many opportunities for winter sports. The miles of paths in Gorkiy Park are frozen over in winter. Here young and old skate, and occasionally the path widens into a rink where racing and figure skating can be practiced. Skiers who find the modest slopes in Lenin Heights or the ski jumps with a maximum of 230 feet not challenging enough, simply take the subway to the outskirts of the city where cross-country ski runs wind through great forests of birch trees. For those who find a swim in an ice hole in the Moskva a bit cold, there is a large open-air swimming pool in the middle of the city. The temperature of the water is maintained at 80 °F all year round, even when air temperatures drop to –40 °F.

63 *Mos-Soviet Theater in Moscow.* A dramatization of Heinrich Böll's *The Clown* is on the bill. Moscow is the cultural center of the Soviet Union, with thirty-eight theaters, numerous concert halls, performances of the Bolshoi Ballet, and eighty-odd movie houses all of which are sold out day in and day out. The ordinary citizen often has to wait months to get tickets; officials and such privileged people as foreigners can get them more easily.

64 *The painter Ilya Sergeievich Glazunov in his Moscow studio.* Glazunov lost his parents during the World War II siege of Leningrad, where he was born in 1930. His art is not, generally speaking, in the school of social realism, and his second large exhibit in the Manege in Moscow, with more than 7,000 visitors daily, was closed down by order of the government four days after it opened. The controversial Glazunov, a passionate collector of icons, is best-known for his portraits. He has painted such varied celebrities as the king of Laos, William Averell Harriman, Luchino Visconti, Gina Lollobrigida, Edgar Faure, Prime Minister Jens Otto Krag of Denmark and his wife, a famous film actress. Since his first exhibition in Moscow in 1957, Glazunov's works have been shown in Warsaw, Rome, Copenhagen, and Paris.

Some of his paintings also hang in private and public collections in the West.

65 *Leo Tolstoy's house in Moscow.* This house — now a very popular museum, which I visited during a snowstorm — is located at 21 Leo Tolstoy Street. When the writer moved here with his family in 1881, he had already achieved world renown for some of his greatest works. Even at the age of sixty, Tolstoy sometimes walked from his summer residence in Yasnaya Polyana to Moscow, a distance of 125 miles.

66 *View through the window into the children's room in Tolstoy's house.* The large park was buried under several feet of snow. While plodding around the house in the storm, I discovered this view into the room of Tolstoy's last child, his son Vanya, who died of scarlet fever when he was only seven years old.

The masses of snow are quite a problem for the Moscow city administration. According to the Bureau of Statistics, an average 28,773,800 cubic yards of snow fall on the streets of Moscow annually. Very early in the morning snow plows begin clearing the streets, driving in formation along the city's broad boulevards.

Traffic in Moscow slows down during the cold season since many motorists store their vehicles for the winter. Antifreeze is a scarce commodity. Those who must be on the road, such as taxi drivers, empty their radiators overnight and fill them up with warm water in the morning.

Driving discipline in the U.S.S.R. could be better. The man behind the wheel rarely takes his foot off the gas pedal when approaching a pedestrian crossing, unless, of course, a policeman happens to be nearby. On the other hand, pedestrians act as if the street belonged to them, not moving out of the way until cars are dangerously close. Such difficulties are the frequent subject of letters to the editor in Russian newspapers. Only the privileged can afford to buy a car. The most popular automobile, the Volga, sells for more than $ 6,700; the average per capita income barely exceeds $ 160 a month. No wonder then that tempers flare when there is a traffic accident and that pedestrian witnesses invariably put the blame on the driver.

It never ceased to amaze me how carefree Russians are with their money and how very hospitable, inviting guests to expensive restaurants, giving generous tips, and throwing a handful of ruble bills on the table when paying. After all, one ruble is worth about $ 1.12 (this was before the U.S. dollar devaluation in 1971). A Russian considers it perfectly reasonable to pay 12 or even 19 rubles for a hotel room in Moscow. However, when I tell him that I have to pay the equivalent in U.S. dollars, in fact 10 percent more, then he finds it positively exorbitant. The official exchange rate at the time was 90 kopeks to a dollar; on the black market, however, a dollar bought four to five times that amount.

Upon my return from Leningrad, I learned that the marine expedition had, after all, been canceled. However, there was talk of setting up a new program under the auspices of the Meteorological Institute to visit a number of weather stations in the Arctic. Aeroflot has a run to Dickson on the Arctic coast. One problem was that flying on from there to Haze Island or to one of the floating ice stations near the North Pole would probably cost more than $ 2,000. Despite the expense, I asked the authorities to go ahead with plans for the project. I was very interested in the success of this venture since I had hoped to experiment with certain ideas that had never before been expressed photographically. I also thought that, with a little luck, I might be able to get color shots of the northern lights in the Arctic winter. Since such plans could not be realized overnight, I decided to fly home again, but not before having elicited the promise that I would be notified by telegraph the moment the flight had been arranged.

Commentary

by Harrison E. Salisbury

I

For 300 years travelers from the West have been making their way to Moscow, seeking to penetrate the enigma that is Russia. The walls of old European libraries are lined with the accounts of those who have made the journey—seldom an easy one, often a dangerous one. If today, in the final decades of the twentieth century, we are still seeking the answer, I think it must be concluded that there is more truth in Winston Churchill's famous epigram, "Russia is a riddle wrapped in a mystery inside an enigma," than the modern generation of computer-armed, systems-oriented scholars have been prepared to concede.

The question and its answer would not loom so urgently were it not for the Soviet Union's vast weight in the world. Our preoccupation constitutes recognition that the U.S.S.R. is not merely a country, a European country if you will (yet, also the largest Asian country) but a continent, as one of its most perceptive historians, V.O. Klyuchevsky, pointed out many decades ago. Russia is so vast that unlike all but two or three other nations in the world it is of itself entire, complete, self-sufficient, an entity quite capable of withdrawing behind its borders and living in sulky isolation for a century or two. But Russia is also a continent which, when stirred, organized, and led can, like a tidal wave, sweep over lesser lands, thrusting 5,000 Siberian miles to the Bering Straits and another 2,000 down the American coast to San Francisco (as it did a scant 150 years ago); surging from behind the Dniester to the boulevards of Paris (as it did after Napoleon); raising the red flag over the Brandenburg Gate (as it did at the end of World War II).

This is the reality of Russia which lies behind the rough rhetoric of a Nikita Khrushchev and the "Brezhnev doctrine" of his clerklike successors, behind the technological miracle of Soviet thermonuclear bombs and intercontinental ballistic missiles, behind Russian spacemen and rockets to Mars, behind the creation from a peasant mass of illiterate "dark people" of a modern industrial state second only to the United States.

Russia packs a powerful punch. When the nation begins to move, the earth trembles and the tremors run from the walls of Peking's Forbidden City to the narrow canyons of Wall Street.

It is sheer mass which gives the Soviet Union such a presence in the world, and only short memories are likely to attribute this to the Soviet era. The nineteenth century was dominated by two great powers in motion—the British Empire and the Russian. We are more aware of the British Empire and the swath it cut through the nineteenth century. But Russia and Britain were locked in toe-to-toe competition for 100 years, and it was this titanic rivalry that shaped the destiny of modern Europe and Asia. Now Britain's empire is scattered to the seven seas, but that of tsarist Russia, partially lost in the Russo-Japanese War and the revolution, today stands remarkably intact, a living monument to the aggressiveness, acquisitiveness, single-minded purpose, and tightfisted self-interest of a succession of Russian rulers whose political system might change from Romanov autocracy to Communist dictatorship but whose territorial objectives and aspirations have varied hardly an iota from Nicholas I to Stalin's heirs. Their eyes are still fixed on Far Eastern hegemony, a Middle Eastern presence (and warm-water ports) and "insurance" along their Central European frontiers.

The creation of the powerful machine which is Russia has been no easy task. It has required iron-willed rulers—Ivan the Terrible, Peter the Great, Catherine the Great, Nicholas I, and, in the Communist era, Lenin and Stalin. Because Russia is more a continent than a country, it has never been easy to defend—the Huns, the Scythians, the Mongols, and other nomadic hordes ravaged the Russian steppe from the east and one great warrior after another—Gustavus Adolphus, Napoleon, Hitler—swept in from the west. No Russian ruler has ever slept in ease and security behind the rose-brick crenellated walls of the Kremlin. The danger of attack—from east or west—has always been there. It still is. And the Russian trudging his endless miles over the grassland sea which he calls the steppe instinctively casts an eye at the far horizon. Who knows what menace may lurk there, who knows when sudden death, pillage, and rape will strike from beyond the low range of the Urals? Or across the boggy marches of the Pripet?

The Russian state has been built—and still is being built—with the sweat, toil, and blood of simple Russian men and women. Never has there been more than a moment of repose before the tasks resume—the sowing of the grain on the endless fields, the mining of the earth's treasures, the cutting of the vast forests, the building of new Pittsburghs, Manchesters, Garys, and Düsseldorfs. To found Petersburg cost Peter the Great the lives of 100,000 subjects. To industrialize the Donets coal fields and the Baku oil fields, Count Sergei Witte exported so much wheat that millions of peasants starved to death. To protect his empire against Hitler's assault, Stalin spent the lives of at least 20 million men, women, and children. Some say the toll ran closer to 30 million or 40 million if overall population losses are compiled. Russia is a lavish land, and its rulers have always spent the blood of their people with a free hand.

II

If there is a key to the Russian character — that of the rulers as well as the ruled — it probably can be found in geography and history — the formlessness of the vast reaches which the Russians inhabit and the shape this gave to their lives. There has always been in Russian life a sense of peril not found in the smaller, river-and-mountain-bound kingdoms of Europe. There castles, moats, fortresses, city walls, and water barriers provided relative safety and security. Not so in Russia. If, as many believe, there is in Russian character more suspicion of the foreigner than is encountered in other peoples, perhaps the reason lies in this. Life experience and history teaches the Russian that the stranger appearing suddenly in his land is more likely than not an enemy — covetous of his fertile fields, his rich cities, his cattle, and his women. So ingrained is this conviction that a succession of Russian rulers, beginning with Ivan the Terrible and coming down to Stalin in our day, have forbidden marriages between Russian women and foreigners. Even Stalin's more enlightened heirs throw every possible obstacle in the way of mixed marriages and often prevent for months and even years the uniting of Russian women with their husbands abroad.

Rare is the Russian who does not find an explanation for this and other chauvinistic traits in the yoke of the Mongols — the 250 years in which the Golden Horde sat on the back of the Russian people, reaping tribute, devastating Russian cities (the equal of any in Europe before the Mongols came in the thirteenth century), and, as Russians still believe, setting the Russian clock two or three centuries behind that of the rest of Europe.

It is in the long years of the dominance of the Golden Horde that Russians find their favorite excuse for backwardness, for sloth, for deception, for tyranny, for cruelty, for the capriciousness of their rulers and the obsequiousness of the ruled, for the sly cunning of the peasant and the crude sadism of an Ivan or a Stalin. The Russian peasant learned to bow low, to fawn, to please his master — but never to betray the hostile thoughts and intentions he concealed behind his impassive face. The Russian princes learned to make the kowtow, to accept the Yarlik (symbol of Mongol rule), to pay their tribute while plotting secretly to fall on their hated Mongol masters. These traits have never vanished from Russian nature.

It was to lift the cultural, social, and technological yoke imposed by the Mongols that Peter the Great launched his terrifying effort to pull boyar-and-muzhik Russia, screaming and digging its heels deep into the black *chernozym,* into the eighteenth century, building St. Petersburg as his famous "window on the west", importing cadres of skilled artisans and engineers to provide the foundations of modern shipbuilding, modern military arts, modern metalworking, outraging his sodden countrymen by hacking off their beards (or making them pay a tax of one ruble per beard) and ripping traditionally oriental caftans from their backs, replacing them with sensible Dutch breeches and jackets.

It was to end this backwardness, this tyranny of ignorance and repression, this wayward lag in Russian public life, that one generation of young Russian intellectuals after another sought throughout the nineteenth century, from 1825 on, to change the system — by peaceful agitation, powerful propaganda, the influence of literate and liberal noblemen, and, when all else failed, finally, by assassination, violence, bombs, organized revolution.

This triumph came in Lenin's revolution of 1917. A new era dawned in Russia. Or so it seemed. From all over the world excited observers flocked to Russia to see the miracle of the new day, the social experiment to end all social experiments, the attempt to bring about in this sad and backward country, massively wounded by World War I, a new order in which man's inhumanity to man would be ended, man's exploitation of man would halt, human values would replace monetary values and idealism would sit on the throne so long occupied by greed and superstition. The great experiment attracted the restless minds of the world. John Reed, not long out of Harvard, was on the scene to witness and record Lenin's triumph. He was a believer. The great radicals of America came — Emma Goldman, Big Bill Haywood, the IWW's, the long-haired aesthetes of Greenwich Village. The Webbs came from England. So did H. G. Wells, who went away skeptical. André Gide came, believed, turned on his belief. Lion Feuchtwanger came and recorded the puristic aspirations which Stalin voiced. Overnight backward peasant Russia strode to the center of the world stage. Every actor stood in the spotlight. New York, London,

Berlin, and Paris watched and waited to see what the shape of the new Utopia might be—what lessons it bore, what hopes and threats it portended.

III

Perhaps no visit to Russia was more symbolic in the contemporary view than that of Lincoln Steffens, the radical muckraker, high priest of American journalism, the great skeptic who had exposed the shabby reality of so many American myths. Steffens came to Russia and proclaimed: "I have seen the future and it works."

Fifty years have passed since Steffens' proud, defiant judgment. Steffens' future is *now*—laid out before our eyes. How does it match his vision? We have seen the death of Lenin and Stalin's rise. Stalin's slaughterhouse politics. Peasants driven into collective farms by the machine gun, the hangman's noose, the prison camp. How many so-called kulaks and their families paid with their lives? To this day no one knows. Possibly 5 million lives directly—that is, shot, executed, or dying en route to exile in Siberia. Possibly another 5 million dead in the famines caused when the peasants killed their livestock and didn't bother to plant the wheat and oats. Then the Stalinist purges. How many lives did they cost? No one in Russia or outside knows the numbers. Possibly 10 million. And another 20 million herded into the slave camps of Siberia, the slave mills of Central Asia, the slave mines of the Arctic. World War II. How many lives? No one knows within 5 or 10 million. The postwar purges? Five million Russian prisoners of war who survived Hitler's Buchenwalds were sent by direct cattle car to Stalin's slave camps in Norilsk and Kolyma. The total population of the Tatar state in Crimea, of four small principalities in the Caucasus, all the ethnic Germans, hundreds of thousands (maybe millions) of Estonians, Lithuanians, Latvians, Ukrainians, Jews, the remnants of the Black Sea Greeks—all these and many, many categories which have not yet come to light—all sent to the camps.

Who were these men and women transported to Siberia—criminals, dangerous enemies of the state? Crude thieves? Slovenly peasants, tramps, prostitutes, itinerants? By no means. They were Aleksandr Solzhenitsyn, the Nobel-prize winning author. They were Andrei Tupolev, the great aircraft designer (some of his finest planes were designed in a KGB prison laboratory). They were diplomats like Ivan Maisky. They were editors, musicians, biologists like Nikolai Vavilov who had headed the Academy of Science, and great generals like Marshal Konstantin Rokossovsky.

This was "the future" which stood around the corner from Steffens' sparkling eyes. Not the future which Steffens thought he saw. Not the future of which 100 years of young Russian idealists dreamed. Not the future which the grimy Petersburg workers thought they were winning on the barricades of 1917, not the comfortable fat life which the peasants thought they were ensuring when they burned down the estates of their masters.

No. This was the reality of Russia as it was under Ivan, under Peter, under Nicholas brought up-to-date. Harsh, cruel, heedless of life, heedless of feeling, rushing onward to destiny without a backward look at the bodies crushed and broken by the iron troika.

Why did it happen? It is questions like this which have tantalized one generation after another of Russians and those who seek to understand Russia. The history of Russia is a succession of questions — questions which are almost beyond answer. From the time of the Decembrist revolt of young officers in 1825 until 1917, the question most frequently asked was "*Chto delat?*" or "What is to be done?" or "What can be done?" or "What should we do?" or "Who is guilty?" These questions haunted the years. They still haunt Russia.

Stalin's answer was never given directly. Once he told Churchill that had he known what a terrible struggle he was entering when he launched the drive for collectivization of agriculture, he would not have done it. Perhaps not, but the brute force he employed was in the great Russian tradition. Peter broke the boyars and cowed the Orthodox Church with just such methods, and Stalin used the same kind of force to industrialize Russia and never had a moment's qualms. The cost of industrialization was paid by the sacrifice of Russians compelled to live for decades in subsistence conditions, working themselves to death, just as they had for the horny-handed early Russian entrepreneurs. Stalin knew no other way to build Russia and, as he once said, "to slacken the pace would mean to lag behind and those who lag behind are beaten.... The history of old Russia consisted of the fact that she was always being beaten.... We are fifty or 100 years behind the advanced countries. We must make good this lag in ten years. Either we do it, or they will crush us."

This is a rationale which all of Stalin's predecessors would have accepted without question—and his successors as well. The sense of being behind, the urgent necessity to catch up, to overtake, to exceed—this was the theme of Stalin's successor, Nikita Khrushchev—to overtake the United States, to produce more steel, more oil, more arms—and also more milk, butter, meat, and eggs.

Khrushchev was shoved off the stage of history by his ambitious and bureaucratic associates. They did not question his goals, but they could not abide his methods, his violation of every rule of gray and somber red tape, his appeal to the masses, his unconcealable tendency toward liberalism. They shouldered the burden of pushing Russia forward and headed onward in the same direction fixed so long before by their tsarist ancestors.

And so today, despite all the changes, despite the substitution of Khrushchev for Stalin and of Brezhnev and Kosygin for Khrushchev, the elemental course of Russia has not changed. The Soviet Union is still being driven forward in heavy industry, the "metal-eaters" still win the priorities, although the pace is a bit slower than thirty years ago. Creature comforts are sacrificed for new chemical and metallurgical plants; rockets and ICBM's go ahead of butter and private motor cars. Still the Soviet Union races onward to overtake and surpass the United States, hardly aware that despite its mad rush the quiet Japanese with their industriousness, their efficiency, their remarkable organizational skills, are on the point of overtaking the Soviet Union from behind.

IV

But the Soviet Union, of course, is not just headlong industrialization and endless human sacrifice. It has, although some Americans are not aware of this, one of the finest and noblest humanitarian traditions of any people. It was forged in the post-Catherine days of Alexander I and Nicholas I and has been maintained unbroken to this day, largely by the poets, philosophers, and writers who have passed the torch of freedom and democracy from one decade to the next.

Alexander Pushkin was the first pure voice of this strain of Russian liberalism, and each following era, down to the present day, has found a successor. The emergence of great figures like Pasternak and Solzhenitsyn was a surprise only to those who had assumed that Stalin's secret police had somehow succeeded where the tsar's Third Section had failed in quenching the last spark of liberty and creativity from the Russian soul. For 100 years the tsar's police struggled with the problem but never won a final victory. Each time they thought they had stamped out the latest quest for human freedom — the Narodniki who tried to carry the message to the simple peasants, the Narodnaya Voltsi who chose the route of political assassination, the Socialist Revolutionaries who carried on the banner of terror, the Marxist groups which finally gave birth to Lenin and his Bolsheviks — each time the police thought they had once more made Russia safe for autocracy, the spark sprang into flame again.

So it has also proved under the Bolsheviks. Stalin killed, exiled, imprisoned, terrorized as no Russian ruler since the time of Ivan the Terrible. But he was not quiet in his grave when the voice of liberal, humanitarian Russia was heard again from the very gates of his terrible prisons. First, Boris Pasternak burst on the world like the explosion of a powerful delayed-action bomb. Then Solzhenitsyn, the very spirit of the camps, a man whose genius had been tempered behind the barbed-wire stockades of the far north and Central Asia. He emerged from the Stalinist camps, his soul and mind intact despite the weakening of his body, with the whole of the terror imprinted upon his genius as characters are imprinted on impermeable tape. He began to speak, and instantly there sounded the ancient tocsins which have always aroused Russia's conscience. He spoke for the indestructibility of man's virtue, for the incorruptibility of man's soul, for the indivisibility of man's faith. He spoke with the moral force of a Tolstoy emerging from the same prison hell which had given Dostoyevsky his torrential force.

No one in the Kremlin, not even Khrushchev, has been able to keep the sound of Solzhenitsyn's indictment from echoing in his ears. It is a voice that cannot be stilled. Nor is it just one improbable survivor of the camps who has spoken up. There are also the voices of the young — the poets like Andrei Voznesensky, Yevgeny Yevtushenko, Bella Akhmadulina. Yevtushenko forced on a reluctant state and nation the ugly truth of Babi Yar and warned that Stalin's ghost may yet rise from his grave and haunt the Soviet land. The fierce words of Voznesensky have consumed the bland hypocrisies of the pedants of the Kremlin. Behind them has marched a brilliant company of editors and older writers — Aleksandr Tvardovsky providing a forum for truth in the magazine *Novy Mir,* Ilya Ehrenburg drawing on half a century of memories to reconstruct the past and correct the Stalinist lies before the moment dims, Konstantin Simonov, a blunt, stubborn force who has refused to cosmeticize World War II. A generation of young revisionist historians managed to get half the story of the Stalin purges and of World War II told before being savagely repressed.

And, miracle of miracles, a genuine democratic political movement, small, hampered, harassed, operating half in the underground, half in the spotlight of international publicity, has sprung into being. It has no real shape, and American politicians would snicker at its simple mechanisms. But it is a political movement, a real one, and it is the first to arise, fresh, principled, courageous, since power passed into the hands of Lenin's Soviet on November 7, 1917. At the heart of the new "Democratic Movement", as its members refer to it, stands the physicist Andrei D. Sakharov, one of the most brilliant of contemporary Soviet scientists, often referred to as the father of the Russian H-bomb. Sakharov first came into public view in 1968 with the publication (abroad) of his "Manifesto", a detailed blueprint for the democratization of life within the Soviet Union and for collaboration between the Soviet Union and the United States with a view to combating collectively the global problems of war, hunger, population, disease, and social welfare. He strongly warned his countrymen against any backward step toward Stalinism. How profoundly Sakharov's "Manifesto" may have affected sentiment within the Soviet government cannot be judged, but each year since 1968 has been marked by a measurable spread in the acceptance of his general views within what the Russians call the "scientific and technological intelligentsia"—that is, the men and women on whom the state is dependent for its continued competitive position in the great power race for military and industrial supremacy. Sakharov himself has grown increasingly bold and active. He issued a second "Manifesto" in 1970, reinforcing his first and making specific his proposals for a gradual transition in the Soviet Union from a Communist dictatorship to an electoral democracy. And he publicly formed a small committee on human rights which has established formal affiliation with human rights groups abroad. Standing with Sakharov on most questions is an impressive group of intellectuals—the great physicists Peter Kapitsa, Igor Y. Tamm, and Mikhail A. Leontovich, editors and writers like Tvardovsky (now dead) and Vladimir D. Dudintsev (author of *Not by Bread Alone*), and the famous twin scientists, Roy Medvedev and Zhores Medvedev. The Medvedevs are the authors of four major works — *The Rise and Fall of T. D. Lysenko* (the Stalinist tsar of biological sciences), *The Medvedev Papers* (a study of internal Soviet censorship and controls exercised over scientists, particularly in contacts with foreigners), *Let History Judge* (the most comprehensive study of Stalin and Stalinism yet to be completed within the Soviet Union), and *A Question of Madness* (a study of the use of psychiatric hospitals for the confinement of political dissenters in the Soviet Union) — which provide an unmatched panorama of the Stalinist and post-Stalinist Soviet Union. None of the works has been published in the U.S.S.R.; each, however, circulates widely in *samizdat* — that is, photocopied or mimeographed manuscripts passed from hand to hand.

These men, in general, believe in the perfectibility of the Soviet system. They believe that the state can be changed and modified to correct its enormous deficiencies.

There are other dissenting groups with different objectives. The most spectacularly successful have been the Jewish dissident groups. The Jewish dissident movement began to gather momentum four or five years ago with broad support among the generalized intelligentsia. Increasingly, Jewish dissidents took a bolder and bolder position, organizing protests, public demonstrations, sit-ins at government offices, petitions, appeals for support in foreign countries — all the apparatus of modern political agitation. The state responded with typical Russian repression. Demonstrators were arrested, petitioners lost their jobs. Soon many were hustled into court and hastily condemned to prison camps. But the movement went forward until, with one of those curious turns which sometimes characterize the most tyrannical of regimes, suddenly in 1971 the Soviet Union began to permit thousands of Jews to emigrate to Israel. Even the leading dissenters were flown back from Siberian camps and put on planes for Vienna and, ultimately, Israel.

Non-Jewish groups have met a harsher fate. An unbroken succession of young poets and writers beginning with Andrei Sinyavsky and Yuri Daniel and Josef Brodsky have been sent off to labor camps which hardly differ from those of Stalin. Many are sent to the infamous Serbsky Psychiatric Institute, operated by the secret police as a kind of modern-day substitute for the concentration camp.

But this is not merely a twentieth-century continuation of the police methods long ago invented under the tsars (Tsar Nicholas I had the nineteenth-century Russian philosopher Pyotor Y. Chaadayev declared insane and confined to his home because of what he regarded as his "radical" political opinions). It clearly reflects the brittleness of the regime, its unwillingness on the one hand to countenance change but its reluctance to return to the full and free application of Stalin-style force in order to hold back the tides of new thought. On his deathbed Nicholas I of Russia, the "iron tsar", said: "As for myself I cannot change—my successor must do as he will." This sentiment may yet be written as an epitaph for the Soviet regime. As Sakharov most forcefully has noted, unless the regime finds ways with which to reinvigorate its intellectual, creative, and scientific life, it cannot hope to stay abreast— let alone gain an advantage—in the tumultuous competition of the great power world.

V

Where lies Russia's future? The question troubles the men of the Kremlin as well as ever-widening circles of intelligentsia, those who protest, those who are disturbed but silent, and even those who resent most violently any basic deviation from the steel-tracked police state erected by Stalin.

What of the people—the masses of the peasants and the hordes of urbanized industrial workers who now for the first time markedly outnumber their rural compatriots? If Khrushchev and his successors are right, the aspiration of the Russian worker is to a more comfortable, luxurious life—a car, an apartment or house of his own, cheaper and better clothing, shorter and less arduous workdays, a chance for a decent vacation and a little leisure. And— except, possibly, for the case of China—no war.

It is difficult as you talk to Russians from one end of the country to the other to find many remnants of revolutionary idealism, of revolutionary fervor, of hopes for a more just and equitable existence. What Khrushchev used to call "goulash communism" seems to be supreme among the workers and the toilers. Nor do they exhibit much sentiment in favor of the dissidents, the liberals, the famous writers and scientists like Pasternak, Solzhenitsyn, and Sakharov. Many of them do not even know the names. They are, quite often, strongly chauvinistic, especially vis-à-vis the Chinese, who are perceived as a dangerous enemy. There is more than a hint of racism in their talk of the "yellow peril". There seems little reason to anticipate much yeast for future change in the Soviet lumpen proletariat.

Not so the youth. You will see young people on the streets of Moscow and in the crude cafes of Siberia and Central Asia. They are bored by ideology, unmoved by the platitudes of the dialectic, interested almost entirely in those phenomena of Western youth which have been imported across their frontiers — the dress, the talk, the dances, the music, and, to a small but increasing extent, the drug culture. They are restless and alienated. Can they be an element of change? Some intellectuals believe so. They believe that below the superficial cynicism of Soviet youth there is fermenting the kind of sentiment which might produce a powerful eruption. They do not believe Soviet youth is immune to all the forces which have influenced and stimulated the youth of other countries in the past decade.

What of the bureaucrats and the vast apparatus which is attached to the state, which lives by the status quo? Here the sentiment for holding on to what each one has, to resisting change because change may mean a loss of status, privilege, or perquisites is intense. Here can be found those who openly yearn for the "strong hand" of Stalin, who dream of a return to rule by pure *diktat,* to enforcement of the state's will by terror and the police.

They have even begun to elaborate a new ideology which closely resembles the repressive ideology of Russia's past — emphasis on "Great Russian culture" (painstaking restoration of Russian historical monuments, the ornaments of the Russian Orthodox Church, icons, the legends of the great Russian rulers), chauvinistic attitudes toward the lesser peoples of the Soviet (the Ukrainians and the peoples of the Caucasus, the Baltic, Central Asia), ever more and more open anti-Semitism (often taking the form of private expressions which are virtually unchanged from those employed by the tsarist anti-Semitic Black Hundreds), emphasis on the great mission of Russia in the world (stated in terms which would have satisfied the most xenophobic of the Romanovs). All of this, for the moment, is purely unofficial, but the sentiments find expression in works by the literary ideologues of the new Slavophile movement like Vsevolod Kochetov.

It may be no coincidence that those who preach the new Great Russian philosophy also inveigh against "liberal" writers and call in chauvinistic terms for a "settlement" with China. And it was these same elements which so enthusiastically supported the Brezhnev intervention in Czechoslovakia.

But there is another force stirring in Russia. This is nationalism—not of the Russians but of peoples like the Georgians, the Kazakhs, the Uzbeks, the Balts, the Azerbaidzhani, and, most importantly, the Ukrainians. In the nineteenth century Russia was called by the young revolutionaries "the prison house of nations". The empire was notorious for its repression of subject peoples. All of this, it was believed, would be changed by revolution. But *plus ça change, plus c'est la même chose*. Today there is not a single lesser partner in the Soviet Union which does not harbor nationalistic resentment and anger against the Great Russianism of Moscow. For decades it was said that such feelings were meaningless. It was inconceivable that the subject peoples would rise against Soviet Moscow as the Poles and the Finns used to rise against the tsars. Today no one is so sure. As the nationalities have watched the success of Jewish agitation against the state, more and more often they have raised the question: If the Jews are permitted to leave for their own Israel, why can we not win our national rights? It is a question loaded with dynamite. While Lenin supported the principle of national sovereignty and, specifically, reserved the right of each constituent republic to secede from the union, no state and no people in Russia have ever done so. Nor would secession be permitted. Only by armed force could it be achieved, and thus far there seems no sign of nationalism on a scale which would make armed uprising a realistic possibility.

What, then? Will the union prevail? One Russian thinks not. Andrei Amalrik, a Russian historian, believes the union will not survive. At some future date—he picks 1984 for symbolic reasons—it will fly apart under the trauma of a devastating war with China. The Ukraine and other major republics will win their independence. The union will survive but only in a truncated state, possibly in the form of a small Stalinist Central Asian federation. Amalrik's vision is too apocalyptic to win many supporters. (He has been condemned to a long term in prison camp for promulgating it.) Yet, as decade after decade passes with no essential change in the narrow, repressive atmosphere of Russia, more and more components of the vast nation accumulate cause for grievance and complaint and almost irresistible strivings for change at just about any cost. Somewhere in the not unforeseeable future the moment may arrive at which the sterile bureaucracy of the routinized state will find itself no longer able to cope with the disparate contentions of a multinational, multisocial populace. It is this factor which causes some students of the Soviet to pay heed to Amalrik's thesis while differing from him in its details.

But the Soviet Union is a tidal nation. Currents move slowly. The revolution of 1917 was a full 100 years in the making. It has now persisted well over half a century. Its forward thrust has put Russia into the most advanced technology which man's mind has yet conceived. Soviet scientists match their colleagues anywhere on earth. No nation is better educated. No nation has a broader panoply of social benefits. No nation has a more simple, well-defined national purpose. From the ancient lands of Kievan Rus to the far-flung outposts of Vladivostok and the fog-shrouded Pacific littoral, Russians toil and slave for the greater glory of their fatherland. If some intellectuals, some poets, some physicists, and a few philosophers question the path the nation has taken and the reality of the distant goal to which it aspires, far more, in all probability, still see Russia, as Gogol did, "like a bold troika that cannot be caught".

"The road smokes beneath you, the bridges tremble, everything retreats and is left behind," Gogol observed. "The onlooker is left amazed at the God-like marvel: is it not lightning thrown from heaven?... The troika races, inspired by God!... But whither, Russia, are you flying? Answer me. She gives no answer. The bell tinkles in wonderful music; torn into shreds, the air thunders and becomes wind; everything flies past, everything on earth, and looking askance, other peoples and kingdoms draw aside and make way for her."

So Russia moves forward today, a wonder to the world and to its own people. But the question hangs in the air: Whither, Russia, are you flying?

The Central Asian Republics

Summer had come again by the time I traveled back to the Soviet Union. The flight to Alma-Ata in the Kazakh S.S.R. took us out of the black earth belt behind Rostov-on-the-Don. Soon after crossing the Volga, we approached Kazakhstan, the land of deserts, steppes, and mountains. Immense fields unfolded beneath us, reminiscent of abstract paintings in shades of brown and yellow. Kazakhstan, second-largest republic in the Soviet Union, also straddles two continents — Europe and Asia. We flew over the dividing line, the Ural River, which empties into the Caspian Sea at Guryev. This city lies on both banks of the river, partly in the western, European, and partly in the eastern, Asian, region of Kazakhstan. In the east and southeast the Altay and Tyan Shan mountains rise out of the earth; here the Khan-Tengri massif looms nearly 23,000 feet high at the converging point of the borders of Kazakhstan, Kirgiz, and China.

Stopover in Karaganda. Next to the entrance of the airport building I noticed some plaques. Oleg translated for me. The official reception for the crew of Vostok VI — cosmonauts Adriyan Nikolayev, Pavel Popovich, and Valentina Tereshkova, the first woman to travel in space — took place here after their touchdown in the vicinity on June 19, 1963. Karaganda Airport serves Baykonyr, the space center of the Soviet Union. Between Karaganda and Alma-Ata we flew over Lake Balkhash, the largest lake in the republic, with a surface area of approximately 6,500 square miles. Kazakhstan is dotted with some 4,000 lakes, two thirds of which contain fresh water. There are also more than 7,000 rivers over 6 miles in length, most of which, however, dry up completely in summer. Since more than two thirds of the area consists of desert and semidesert, the enormous underground supply of fresh water is of great significance for the future of this region. It is estimated that these resources amount to nearly 10 trillion cubic yards.

The Kazakh Republic is extraordinarily rich in energy resources. Coal occurs in more than 100 deposits, said to contain a total of more than 40 billion tons; oil deposits amount to over 5 billion tons. Scientists estimate that 6 percent of the world's known mineral resources are to be found in Kazakhstan.

Night had fallen when we landed in Alma-Ata. The time difference between here and Moscow, 2,500 miles away, is four hours. The hotel had not yet received our telegraphed reservations. Alma-Ata, 2,600 feet above sea level, capital of the Kazakh Republic, has a population of about 700,000. Sixty factories and thirteen large combines are concentrated here, producing one fourth of all foodstuffs in the republic.

67 *Eternal snows above Alma-Ata.* The snowcapped spurs of the awesome Tyan Shan massif, which forms the border with China, rise straight out of the plains south of the city.

68 *Flock of sheep near Alma-Ata.* Centuries ago, nomads, ancestors of the Kazakhs, already trekked across the endless steppes and pasture lands where today more than 500 *sovkhozes* for sheep, the principal livestock of the country, have been established. (A *sovkhoz* is state-owned agricultural land.) A great many new sheep-breeding *sovkhozes* are planned to increase the stock to 40 million.

69 / 70 *At the horse festival in Alma-Ata.* Riders from all over the nation converge in Alma-Ata to participate in the competition. A colorful parade of the various ethnic groups is followed by races and contests. The Central Asians—the Tadzhik in white shirts and the Armenians in black—were showered with applause during the "fur cap game". On either end of the playing field stands a high pole topped by a ring about 16 inches in diameter. The referee throws a cap into the air, and each team tries to catch it. A player is allowed to keep the cap in his possession a maximum of three

seconds. The object is to throw the cap through the ring, which scores one point.

I bought apples—big, beautiful, tasty apples—at a fruit stand for half a ruble a piece (55 cents). People flocked to buy this fruit grown in and around Alma-Ata, the city of apples, literally the "father of apples".

71 *In the textile combine of Alma-Ata.* This enormous new plant is still in the process of expansion. The textile industry in the Soviet Union plays a very important role since textiles, particularly inexpensive cottons, are being exported in increasing quantities, mainly to the Third World. In 1965, for example, more than 10 billion square yards of cotton cloth were manufactured.

When we arrived at the airport to fly on to Tashkent, the woman at the check-in counter asked me what was in my metal suitcases. Photographic equipment, Oleg replied. She told us that transporting such metal cases was against regulations. Oleg was rather annoyed. "Show me your regulations," he said, "or take me to your superior so that he can explain this nonsense to me." We took the cases with us as we had always done before.

An Ilyushin 18 carried us to Tashkent in one and a half hours. It was a constant source of wonder to me that every flight was fully booked and people acted as nonchalantly as if they were taking the bus.

Aeroflot publishes schedules for international flights but not for domestic runs. Although flight information is occasionally posted on the wall in airport buildings, one usually has to inquire about connecting flights. This does not generally concern the Western visitor because Intourist makes all the arrangements. However, since we were on our own, Oleg took care of these things.

Tashkent, with more than a million inhabitants, is the capital of the Uzbek Republic and home of one of Russia's most important

airports, which connects with places all over the world. Nevertheless, checking out our baggage was a grueling experience. Passengers waited in line in front of a wooden partition until a truck piled high with baggage drove into the shed. As soon as an official opened a narrow door, people pushed through it, charged toward the truck, and started grabbing at the baggage. Then everyone had to force his way out again past the same official, who compared the numbers on the tickets with those on the suitcases. We recovered from this experience at the airport restaurant over a glass of fresh kefir, a creamy sour-milk beverage known in the Caucasus, southern Russia, and Siberia. It is made of fermented mare's milk.

72 *Bazaar in the old part of Tashkent.* Old Uzbek men and women wearing their characteristic headgear, the *tyubeteyka*, sit under simply constructed sun roofs surrounded by mountains of melons and baskets brimming over with fruit. Donkeys pull heavily loaded carts through the narrow lanes, the smell of freshly cooked shashlik hovers in the air; it is a truly oriental atmosphere. The fruit is excellent but expensive, considering that it is locally grown. Beautiful apples and pears can cost as much as a ruble a pound.

73 *Teahouse in Tashkent.* Half inside and half outside, shaded by trees, stand low tables covered with rugs. The men remove their shoes and sit here "Turkish style" drinking green tea.

74
75 *Reconstruction in Tashkent.* On April 26, 1966, Tashkent suffered a devastating earthquake which ravaged some 21,525,000 square feet of housing and left more than 75,000 families homeless. I never was able to find out, however, how many lives were lost in this catastrophe. Tashkent is still one vast construction site; countless new buildings, apartment houses, industrial plants, and business offices are springing up all over the city. Fifty-four million square feet of new housing have already been completed.

76 *Modern buildings in the center of Tashkent.* The entire Soviet Union was involved in the reconstruction of Tashkent. Building materials, technical equipment, foodstuffs, and medical supplies poured into the city from every corner of the nation. Kiev, for example, shipped ten construction brigades; in fact, nearly all the republics and major cities sent people and building materials as their contribution to the shattered city.

In the center of Tashkent I focused on the interesting display of a street photographer. He pounced on me and categorically forbade me to take a picture. Oleg thought that he may have felt I wanted to make fun of his "bad" photographs.

Taxis in the Soviet Union are relatively inexpensive. A very nice young taxi driver took us about the city all day long. Once we stopped for over two hours in a section where new construction was going up. Oleg doubted that the driver would wait for us such a long time. Yet he did. In the evening when I tried to give him the tip he deserved, he refused politely but firmly.

Samarkand

The half-hour flight from Tashkent to Samarkand took us over vast barren steppes. Shortly before landing we flew over a historical site, the observatory of Ulug-Beg, famous astronomer and mathematician who was a grandson of Timur (Timur-i-Läng or Tamerlane). Astronomers from both the Orient and the Occident made their observations here for many centuries, basing their calculations on tables that had been devised by Ulug-Beg.

Samarkand ranks with Babylon, Thebes, Athens, and Rome as one of the great cultural centers of the ancient world. Legend has it that Samarkand was founded over 5,000 years ago by King Aphrosiab. First mention is made of Maracanda, as the city was called by ancient chroniclers, in the year 329 B.C. Early poets of Samarkand, where every stone has historical significance, have called the city Eden of the Orient, Light of the Globe, Precious Pearl of the World. Archaeologists have uncovered graves in the environs which date back 100,000 years. The skull and bones of a "Neanderthal" man have been discovered in southern Uzbekistan, and traces of prehistoric man have also been unearthed near Tashkent. Furthermore, pottery dating from 3000 B.C. as well as remains of houses and irrigation ditches from about 1000 B.C. have been excavated on the lower reaches of the Amu-Darya.

The history of Central Asia is a sequence of uninterrupted wars and conquests. Alexander the Great defeated the Persian Empire in 330 B.C. In the sixth century A.D. the Turks dominated Central Asia; in the seventh and eighth centuries the region was conquered by the Arabs; in the tenth century the Turks ruled once again. At that time Central Asia became known as Turkestan, a name that survived until the 1920's.

The peoples of Central Asia experienced the most disastrous invasion of their lands when the hordes of Genghis Khan mercilessly pillaged the countryside and slaughtered almost the entire population (1219–1221). The region then lay in twilight for more than a century until Timur (1336–1405), the great potentate and con-

queror, created a new empire with Samarkand as the capital. Under Timur's rule architecture, science, and the arts flourished in old Samarkand; mausoleums commemorating many renowned representatives of this dynasty are preserved to this day.

77 *Registan Square in Samarkand with minaret and dome of the Shir-Dar Madrasah.* For centuries this square was the focal point of the town where the faithful came to pray and heralds proclaimed events of importance. Registan Square is flanked on three sides by the Ulug-Beg, Shir-Dar, and Tillya-Kari *madrasahs* (Koran schools). The construction of these magnificent edifices was begun in the fifteenth century during the reign of Ulug-Beg.

Of the 11 million inhabitants of Uzbekistan more than 60 percent are actually Uzbeks, a Turkic people whose history is closely interwoven with that of their neighbors, the Kazakhs, Kirgiz, and Turkmen. The Uzbek national costume consists of billowing trousers and a tunic-like garment worn ankle-length by women and just below the waist by men. Over this the people wear a brightly patterned cloak, and on their heads a small round cap, the *tyubeteyka*. The men also wrap a turban around the cap. This traditional apparel in the framework of the ancient monuments creates an enchanting impression of oriental splendor. However, the majority of the people now dress in Western clothes.

78 *Shah-i-Zind Mausoleums in Samarkand.* This group of buildings, interconnected by a narrow passage, lies on the northern edge of Samarkand. The monuments bear witness to a resplendent past with their carved and glazed terra-cotta tiles, painted majolica, and beautiful mosaics of glazed bricks. Their elegance and diversity of form are unparalleled in Samarkand.

The Gur Emir Mausoleum, closer to the center of the city, is one of the most magnificent examples of Uzbek architecture. The

octagonal structure, surmounted by a ribbed, light blue dome, has been restored to its original splendor. It was built by Timur as a tomb for his grandson and heir to the throne, Muhammad Sultan, who fell during a campaign in Asia Minor in 1403. Timur, who died shortly afterward in 1405, was also interred here. In time the mausoleum became the family tomb of the Tamurids. Two of Timur's sons and his grandson, Ulug-Beg, who died in 1449, are buried here as well.

79 *At the market in Samarkand.* An old woman sat at her crude
80 stand selling flat loaves of bread; another peddler was hawking chickens. Next to them was a stand displaying exquisite fruit. Uzbekistan is known for its orchards and viticulture. Many varieties of apples, peaches, sour cherries, pears, and quinces grow here. The pomegranate tree is grown, too, although its fruit is very sensitive to the cold. Temperatures in Uzbekistan range from –4 °F in winter to searing heat in summer — the highest temperature in the U.S.S.R., 121.8 °F, was recorded in Termez, south of Samarkand. Nevertheless, experimental stations have succeeded in cultivating a pomegranate variety which is capable of withstanding such extremes. The juice of the pomegranate has long been believed to possess healing powers. It is still used today as a home remedy for various ills.
Oleg and I bought a flat bread, pressed some warm pieces of freshly roasted shashlik into it, and for 30 kopeks purchased a watermelon that we had cut in half for us. This snack not only tasted delicious, it also cost next to nothing.

On the way to the hotel a little urchin greeted us with "Heil, Hitler". I was astonished. Oleg was visibly annoyed. He wanted to explain the meaning of these words to the little boy, but the child scampered off. We suspected that this had been the doing of a German tourist.

81 *In the streets of Samarkand.* Samarkand is notable not only for its unforgettable architectural monuments of the past; modern developments are also very much in evidence. Colleges, research institutes, industrial plants, apartment buildings, and administrative and cultural centers give an added dimension to this ancient town Central. Asia is a paradise for photographers not only because of the splendid historical buildings and the eternally blue sky, but also because nobody seems to mind the photographer. People never demand baksheesh, a custom which is a plague in other Muslim countries.

We next flew on to Bukhara, which took forty minutes in the small Antonov 24 B. Aeroflot pilots receive excellent training, and service on Intourist flights is more than adequate. However, landing maneuvers, especially in smaller airplanes, are far from pleasant. The aircraft often descends to landing altitude as much as 25 to 30 miles before reaching the runway, and, of course, it is buffeted about if there are strong winds.

Bukhara — Kara-Kum — Ashkhabad

For many centuries Bukhara was no less renowned than Samarkand. The city lies in the Zeravshan Valley on the southern edge of the Kyzyl-Kum, one of Asia's largest deserts. All the major caravan routes once converged on Bukhara, which lent its name to the rugs that were brought to market here from the remotest corners of the Kyzyl-Kum. At the height of its prosperity under Samanid rule in the tenth century, the city had a population of half a million; in 1962 the population was 84,000.

The tourist is welcomed by a wealth of splendid ancient oriental monuments. Standing at dusk before the long city walls in the west and looking toward the mosques and minarets, he finds himself transported into the enchanting atmosphere of the Arabian Nights. The Kalyan Minaret, built in 1127, towers over all the other buildings. From its top the muezzin once called the faithful to prayer. The structure also served as a lookout for approaching enemies and as a lighthouse, illuminated by a fire to guide caravans in the desert. Bukhara more than any other city in Central Asia has retained the imprint of the ancient Orient; the character of the town is perfectly homogeneous.

82 *Mosque with four minarets in Bukhara.* The mosque is made of yellow bricks with glazed blue-green tiles on the domed minarets — a most striking color against the radiant blue of the sky. The entrances to the mosque are all pointed arches.

83 *Domed buildings in Bukhara.* The large squares in Bukhara are bordered by massive domed buildings. Three such structures from the ancient bazaar have survived. Jewelry was sold in one; coin dealers did business in another; and the third was occupied by money changers. Today tourists stroll through this vaulted indoor market to buy souvenirs. Bukhara is still famous for its gold-embroidered clothes, bags and caps, and filigree jewelry.

84 *Girl of the Young Pioneers in Bukhara.* Uzbek girls usually wear their heavy black hair in two thick braids, although the littler girls sometimes have as many as twenty tiny braids. Children in Central Asia no longer have a great deal of faith in the religion of their parents. They believe in Lenin and in socialism. Khrushchev once told them, "We have even launched Gagarin into outer space, but he did not see God there."

85 *Old man beneath hammer and sickle in Bukhara.* The aged sit in the shade and doze or gossip; their manner reflects contentment and philosophical serenity. What do they care about the Lunakhod moonmobile, planned economy, or higher politics....

New industry has been established here; soon more than a trillion cubic feet of natural gas will be pumped out of Bukhara annually. Pipelines to Tashkent and the Urals have already been completed.

We were unable to obtain permits to take the Central Asian railroad from Bukhara to Ashkhabad, and since direct air traffic had been discontinued for some time, we had to fly via Tashkent — about three times the direct distance. The air traffic is extraordinary; six planes in both directions travel between Bukhara and Tashkent daily.

On the way to Ashkhabad we flew over the Amu-Darya River, the most important waterway, separating the Kyzyl-Kum and Kara-Kum deserts, forming a portion of the border between Uzbekistan and Turkestan, and emptying into the Aral Sea. The Amu-Darya is a mighty, and also a moody river. It is said to carry four times as much fertile silt as the Nile. Sandbars, a constantly changing riverbed, and erosion along the banks of the river impede shipping and irrigation. The immense Kara-Kum Desert lies to the west of the Amu-Darya. It was a pity that taking pictures from the airplane was not allowed, because the Antonov

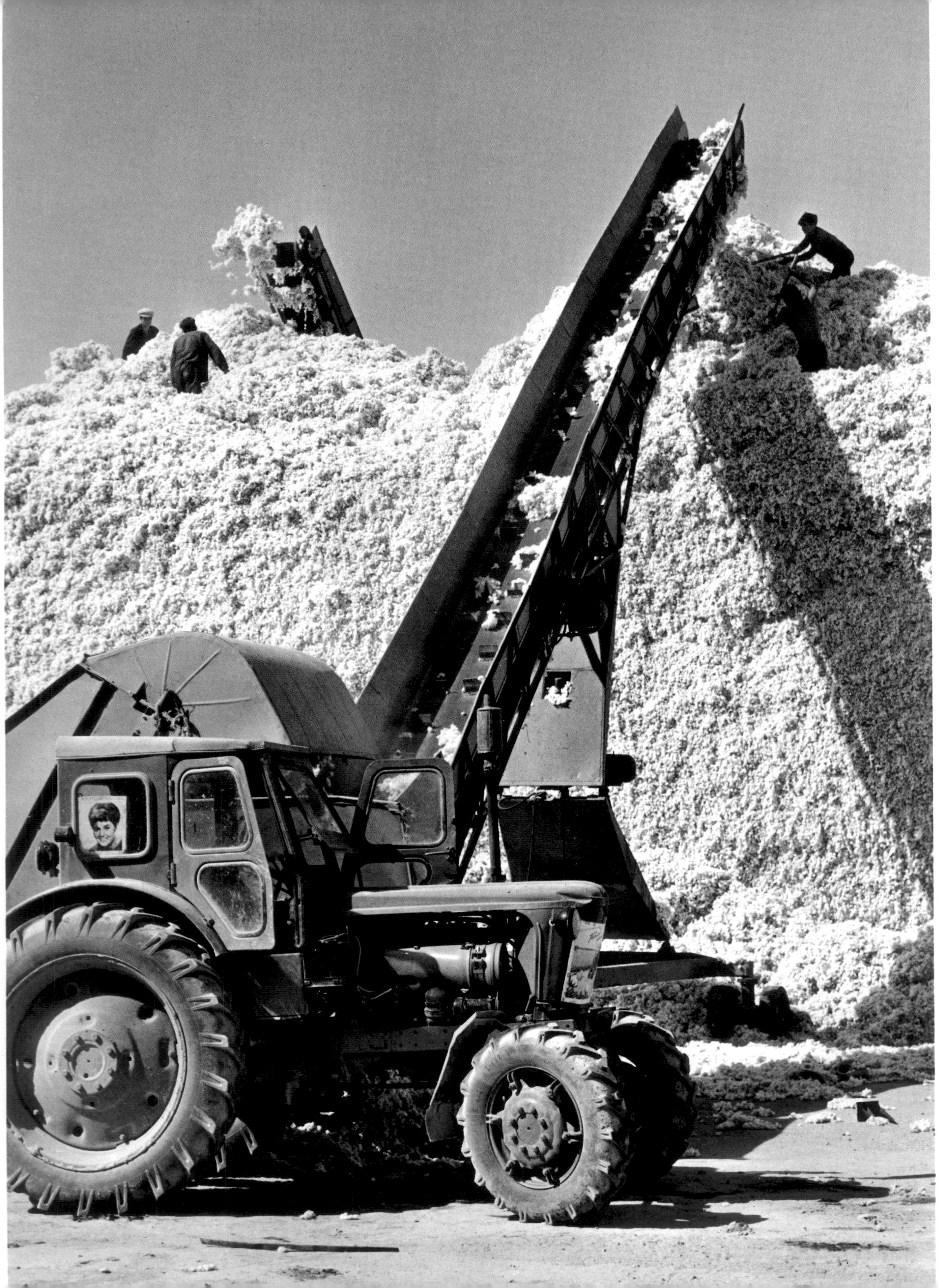

24, a high-wing aircraft, afforded a breathtaking panorama of the parched yellow-gray-brown desert landscape. Shortly before landing in Ashkhabad we flew over the Kara-Kum Canal, our next destination.

A taxi took us along a perfectly straight road to our hotel in the center of the city. "It is the longest and most beautiful stretch of straight road in the world," our driver explained. The road was less than 9 miles long.

86 *Meeting at the Soviet-Turkmenistan Sovkhoz in Ashkhabad.* State-owned agricultural land is called a *sovkhoz,* whereas land combined to form a collectively owned agricultural unit farmed by the original owners is called a *kolkhoz.* Bowls overflowing with exquisite grapes stood on the table. At the head of the table sat Muratberdi Sopier, manager of the *sovkhoz,* who briefed us on the Soviet-Turkmenistan, which employs some 4,000 people.

Among other things we learned that since the completion of the first two stages of the canal approximately 1,000,000 tons of raw cotton, 100,000 tons of grain, more than 700,000 tons of feed, as well as enormous quantities of fruit, have been gleaned from the irrigated lands, some 600,000 acres, 250,000 of which are newly won lands.

"We owe all this to the life-giving water of the Kara-Kum Canal, without which the desert would be a merciless, death-bringing oven," the manager said. Turkmenistan, the hottest republic in the U.S.S.R., has very little water. The manager told us the following legend: "When Allah divided up the earth, the Turkmenian delegate was standing near the beginning of the line. Thus he was given a great deal of land. When the sun was divided up, he was even further in front and was given nearly all of the sun. But when the water was divided up, he was now unfortunately at the end of the line and was given only the meager remains."

87 *Cotton harvest at the Forty Years Turkmenistan Sovkhoz in Ashkhabad.* On the way to these gigantic rectangular mountains of cotton, we saw the picking machines at work on the immense fields. Although it was September, it was still very hot.

We had received special permission to travel through the Kara-Kum Desert. We flew east a few hundred miles to the Mary Oasis. The manager of the new airport introduced us to a Turkmen, Muhammad Gazitov, assistant director of that portion of the Kara-Kum Canal. In a Russian jeep, known as the Gazik, we drove west some 30 miles to the canal, where a small modern hydrofoil was waiting.

The speedy boat soon took the five of us out of the built-up districts. As we traveled upstream, we passed by smaller freighters. After some 30 miles we were surrounded by orange desert sands as far as the eye could reach.

88 *Kara-Kum Canal 30 miles beyond Mary.* We climbed ashore up picturesque dunes bordering the canal. What a magnificent sight: the sparkling azure ribbon of the canal winding its way through the orange-yellow desert and finally vanishing into the horizon!

It took six years to build the 500-mile canal, a formidable technical achievement. The first section begins at the Amu-Darya River, branches off at Kerki, and flows to the Mary Oasis; the second takes the canal from Mary to Ashkhabad; and the third, which is still under construction, will extend to the Caspian Sea. The building of the canal, miles from roads and from any other transportation facilities, has been a major undertaking in this torrid region of the Soviet Union where temperatures may rise to 122 °F and the sand itself can get as hot as 167 °F. Sandstorms sweeping across the vast bleak desert further complicate working conditions for man and machine. Sitting in a comfortable boat where I could simply lean over the edge to dip a glass of fresh, clear drinking water, I was struck by the extraordinary significance of this achievement.

89 *Camel caravan along the Kara-Kum Canal.*   On our return journey we encountered this caravan of some forty camels. Three women seated on donkeys took up the rear to make sure that none of the animals strayed off. What a contrast to the northern regions of the Soviet Union! I asked our guides to stop the boat and tried to run ahead of the caravan in order to photograph the unusual scene on land as well.

We docked at a station near a few buildings. Tables and chairs stood in the shade of some trees — a simple and novel restaurant. Mr. Gazitov, the assistant director, invited us for lunch. First we were served an enormous bowl of soup and meat. It tasted superb. Five tumblers were filled to the brim with vodka … toasts were drunk to the country, the canal, and to friendship. Having downed this huge quantity of liquor, I felt as if I were burning up inside. Too late I realized that I would have done well to have followed up with a water chaser.
The soup alone would have been quite enough for me. What followed defies description. Fried fish, an enormous shashlik, steamed tomatoes, and a Turkmen pilaf, a rice dish with meat, carrots, and fruit. Everything was eaten with the fingers. But time was pressing. A warm, heartfelt farewell, and we took our leave — by boat to the jeep, by jeep to Mary, and finally by plane back to Ashkhabad.

90 *A Turkmen in the streets of Ashkhabad.*   Ashkhabad, capital of Turkmenistan, was devastated by an earthquake on August 6, 1948. The population now exceeds 250,000. With the advent of the Kara-Kum Canal, the city has been transformed into a great flourishing garden.

We flew back to Moscow. Once more we saw below us the Kara-Kum, the black desert. Although it took me several days to recover from the effects of the vodka, my experiences in Central Asia remain unforgettably beautiful.

Siberia

While preparing for my trip to Siberia, I came across Traugott von Stackelberg's fascinating book, *Geliebtes Sibirien* ("Beloved Siberia"), published by Neske in 1951. The author, a member of the Baltic nobility, was banished to Siberia in the days of the tsars. He spent many years there and attained, despite his exile, a profound inner freedom. Stackelberg's memoirs of Siberia include the most beautiful descriptions I have ever read of this region, so very far removed from anything that most of us have known. His vivid account of the ice breakup on the Angara River near Boguchany evokes awesome images of the primeval forces which rage in Siberian rivers in spring. Inspired by this book, I set to work on planning my trip to Siberia with great energy. I discovered that Traugott von Stackelberg was a practicing physician in southern Germany near the Swiss border and went to visit him. Still active and open to new ideas at the age of seventy-nine, Dr. von Stackelberg was delighted with my plans for a photographic work and offered me his support. We toyed with the idea of traveling to Siberia together, to Boguchansk, today known as Boguchany, where Stackelberg had spent the greater part of his exile.

However, I had to give my summer program for Siberia priority and to prevail upon the authorities to approve it. I had already managed to secure special permits for some areas that are normally closed, but I was still waiting for permission to drive through a number of other places on our itinerary, some of which would have been the envy of experts on the Soviet Union: Tyumen, Tobolsk, Khanty-Mansiysk, Tiksi, Pevek, Mirnyy, Verkhoyansk, and Vladivostok. The long-awaited replies were disappointing. Tiksi and Pevek telegraphed refusals. Military maneuvers, which according to *Pravda* were scheduled to take place in the Arctic Zone, had presumably thwarted our plans. Nevertheless, I decided to travel to Siberia, even with a shortened program.

Akademgorodok — Irkutsk — Bratsk

From the Domodedovo Airport about 30 miles from the center of Moscow, we took a Tu-114 jet to Novosibirsk, covering the distance of some 2,000 miles in about three and a half hours. Here we had to set our watches ahead four hours. The journey continued immediately by car to Akademgorodok, 25 miles from Novosibirsk.

91 *Akademgorodok, city of science in Siberia.* The modern city is built in the middle of the endless birch forests of the taiga. Construction was begun in 1958, and by the early 1970's the city had a population of 50,000. Nearly 4,000 students selected from all over the Soviet Union study here in numerous excellently equipped technical and scientific institutes, where they are instructed by outstanding scientists and technicians in problems of large-scale research. The dreams of progressive scientists in the West have virtually become reality here. There are only three students for every professor, and even the most famous research scientists do not consider it beneath their dignity to teach those who will one day take their places. The intellectual elite have left their imprint on this research city; everything is expansive and spacious. The shopping center offers all one could wish for, as the government is interested in making life in the isolation of Siberia as pleasant as possible.

92 *Mikhail Alexeyvich Lavrentyev, scientist and founder of Akademgorodok.* It was his idea to combine the natural-science-oriented university of the "Academic City" with specialized schools for education and advanced studies in mathematics, physics, chemistry, and other sciences. According to Lavrentyev, "The university has lagged behind the progress of the sciences." This dynamic seventy-year-old gentleman conducted us himself on a tour of the research facilities.

93 *Research laboratory in Akademgorodok.* There are sixteen institutes

for a variety of disciplines including nuclear physics, mathematics, geophysics, automation, electrometry, chemistry, and biology. At work in these institutes are fifty members of the Soviet Academy of Sciences, 125 professors, and over 1,000 candidates for the equivalent of our doctoral degree, who have completed their university studies and are preparing for a career in research or teaching.

94 *Data-processing center in Akademgorodok.* Although this computer, model MH-14, is housed at the Institute of Mathematics, it also serves other fields of research.

We returned to Novosibirsk, the largest city east of the Urals, with 1,161,000 inhabitants, and the economic and cultural hub of Siberia. The Trans-Siberian Railroad crosses the Ob River here. Novosibirsk, an important railway center, is the terminus for the Turksib, the railway line between Siberia and Central Asia. Concentrated in and around this metropolis are a harbor and airport, a university and several colleges, the spacious National Library, a branch of the Academy of Sciences, shipyards, meat combines, and factories for motor vehicles, turbines, machines, leather goods, textiles, precision tools, measuring instruments, and chemical and pharmaceutical products.

Irkutsk, which had a population of 420,000 in 1967, lies 870 miles east of Novosibirsk. Founded in 1661 as a military stronghold, it soon became a transshipping center in the Russian trade with China and Mongolia. For centuries this city was also the involuntary home of exiles, criminals, revolutionaries, and prisoners of war. Many of the explorers who opened up Siberia started out from Irkutsk.
Because of the constant threat of earthquakes, structures in the spacious center of the city — administrative offices, museums, the theater, university buildings — are never more than a few stories

92

93

98

97

high. The construction of a hydroelectric power plant (1956, capacity 660,000 kilowatts) gave great impetus to Irkutsk, since it attracted heavy industry, woodworking industries, textile industries, and food-processing plants. Furthermore, the power station served as the principal source of energy during the construction of the enormous Bratsk Dam on the Angara River.

We made the acquaintance of Professor Mikhail Mikhailovich Odimtsev at the Geological Institute of the Academy of Sciences, who offered us his assistance in planning an extensive boat tour on Lake Baykal and also wrote introductions for us to use on our visits to Mirnyy and other places.

95 *New construction in Irkutsk.* From a distance the new housing developments make a most imposing impression, but closer inspection reveals their deficiencies and imperfections. Of course, the primary consideration is to get a roof over everyone's head. However, one would perhaps be less tempted to make comparisons with the West were it not for the official statements, which emphasize the quality and thorough workmanship that have gone into the construction.

96 *Window of an old house in Irkutsk.* These charming rustic dwellings will probably soon have to give way to progress. It is still a pleasure to see with what love the builder of old devoted himself to ornamented details which embellish even such a functional element as a window shutter.

97 *Backyard in Irkutsk.* Most of these cabins have neither running water nor electricity. It would not be surprising if the occupants did not appreciate the "quaintness" that we find so attractive. The old woman living here wondered why I photographed her old house, which she no doubt would have been perfectly content to have seen torn down long ago.

98 *Cosmonaut Konstantin Feoktistov from Voshod I.* We met him by chance in the airport bar because our flight from Irkutsk to Bratsk had been delayed owing to bad weather. He and Doctor Boris Yegorov, up to now the only physician who has ever participated in a space flight, both wear glasses. When once asked if this was not unusual for cosmonauts, Yegorov is said to have replied: "Not at all. After all we fly in comfortable sports clothes, too."

99 *In a kindergarten at Bratsk.*

100 *Bratsk Dam on the Angara.* The dam, 2,625 feet long and 416 feet high, is built between protruding cliffs of basalt and backs up the river for 313 miles, creating a reservoir, the Sea of Bratsk, which is more than four times the size of Lake Champlain.

101 *Turbine bay at the Bratsk power plant.* Twenty turbines, made in Novosibirsk, produce 20 billion kilowatts of electricity annually. The plant, said to have cost over $ 700 million, is expected to be amortized in only a few years. Until recently Bratsk was the largest power plant in the world; however, two still larger Siberian plants are now under construction or already in partial operation.

From Bratsk we were to fly in a small aircraft to a lumber combine. I was looking forward to this undertaking as I had secretly hoped to obtain permission to photograph from the air. This would have been a good opportunity to capture the gigantic Siberian taiga with the Angara River flowing through the vast unbroken forest. Unfortunately, the flight was canceled owing to bad weather; we flew back to Irkutsk.

Baykal

Almost every tourist who goes to Irkutsk, by plane or on the Trans-Siberian Railway, also visits Lake Baykal—a must in the official Intourist travel program. The goal of this excursion is always the village of Listvyanka on the western shores of Baykal, near the point where the Angara River leaves the lake. Listvyanka, easily accessible by car, is also the terminus for the "rockets", as the modern hydrofoils are called, which transport visitors from Irkutsk the 36 miles up the Angara to Lake Baykal. However, I wanted to see something more of the lake than the hurried tourist who generally lunches at a restaurant near the dock and returns to Irkutsk a few hours later. I wanted to spend at least one night on the lake. Therefore, I was very pleased when Professor Odimtsev offered us the use for a few days of one of the boats which are at the disposal of the Institute to conduct scientific investigations on Lake Baykal.

By taxi we drove the 45 miles to Listvyanka along a good road through forests of birch and pine. In the fishing villages along the Angara, each family usually has a log cabin to live in, a barn a little way off, a storage shed, and a bathhouse. This pattern— typical of Siberia—has not changed since the first pioneers settled here. Should the living quarters be razed by fire, the family can at least find minimal protection against the merciless winter cold by taking refuge in the barn.

In Listvyanka we reported, as agreed, to the director of the Limnological Institute with its permanent exhibition of the fauna and geology of Lake Baykal. The director accompanied us to the small harbor and down to the cutter *Academician Bardin*, named after a famous metallurgist. We were introduced to Captain Vadim Leshkevich, the four-man crew, and the machinist's wife, Gala, who was to cook. Gala told us not to buy any food since we could eat with them if we wished. Nevertheless, we returned to the restaurant to buy a bottle of cognac for the crew.

102 *The cutter* Academician Bardin *in a cove on Lake Baykal.* We sailed north all day long, miles from civilization. In the evening we moored the boat for the night at a convenient spot along the shore. With no little effort Oleg and I climbed up the steep thickly wooded embankment carpeted with houseleek and countless varieties of moss and flowers, which permeated the cool evening air with their wonderful earthy fragrance.

We returned to the boat before it was completely dark. Gala had made up the cabin for us during our absence. However, it was impossible to sleep; swarms of mosquitoes descended upon me, eating me alive, not in the least perturbed by my insect spray. Strangely enough the little beasts ignored Oleg.

My alarm went off shortly after 4 A.M. A quick glance at the sky—it was crystal clear. Loaded down with telephoto equipment and a tripod, we struggled up the embankment. Once on top I found a suitable location with an unobstructed view over the boundless lake. I had ample time to prepare for the sunrise.

103 *Sunrise on Lake Baykal.* Soon the first rays of the sun sparkled on the horizon; the fiery red ball rose through the layers of the atmosphere. Its weirdly distorted, constantly changing shape grew ever rounder and brighter until it lost its incomparable colors. The small line with dots on the right of the photograph is a floating tree trunk with three birds resting on it.

Lake Baykal—the name, of Tatar origin, means "rich lake" (rich in fish)—lies 1,495 feet above sea level. It is close to 400 miles long, between 18 and 45 miles wide, and 5,700 feet deep. It is, in fact, the deepest and largest freshwater basin in the world, containing some 30,100,000 cubic feet of water. The temperature of the water remains at a relatively constant 39 °F all year round. Only the surface temperature of the lake varies, rising to about 50 °F during the summer months and freezing over from De-

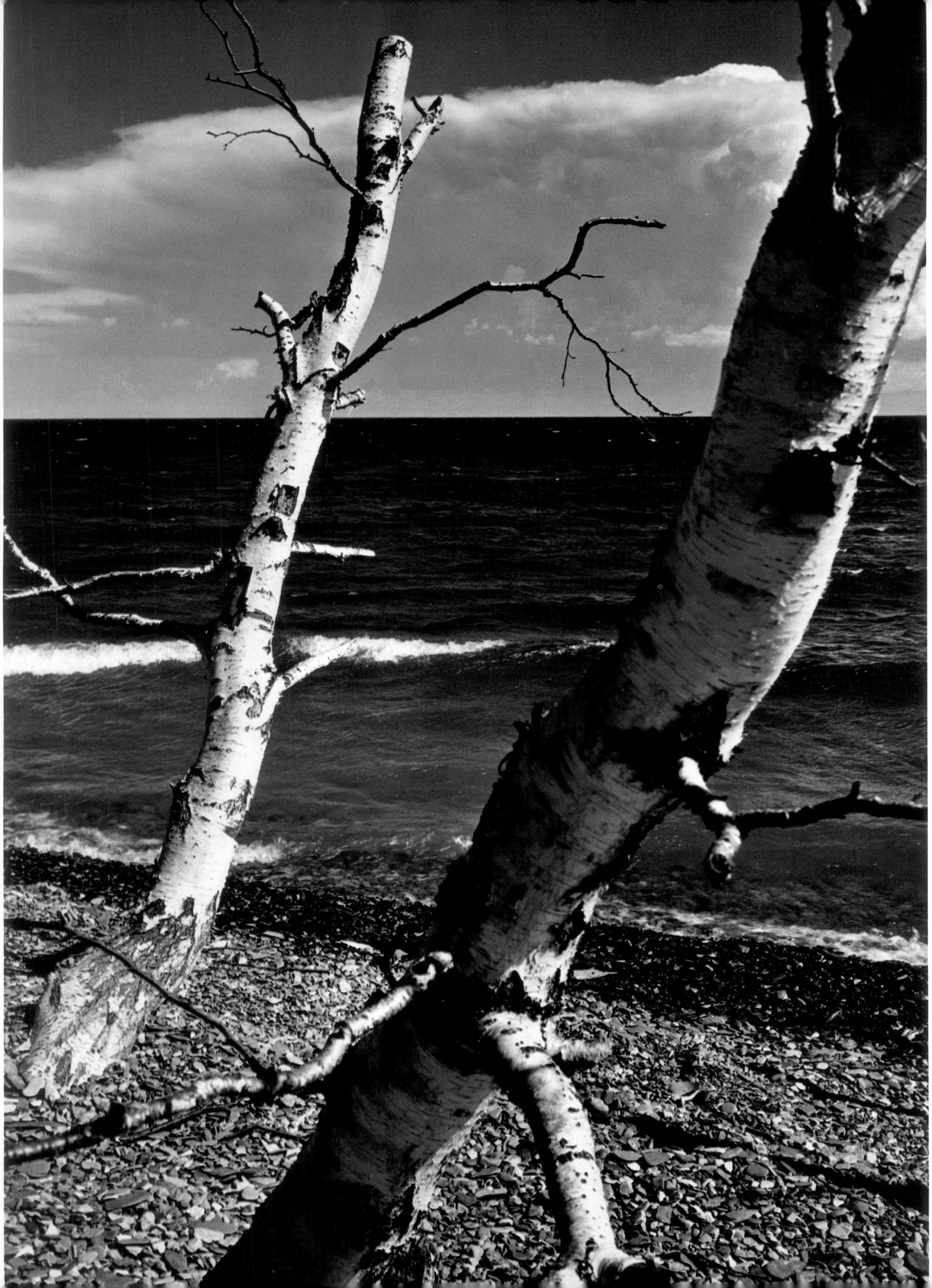

cember to May. Some 330 rivers and streams flow into the lake, which is alive with more than 1,000 varieties of water fauna. A good half of these have never been found elsewhere: the *omul*, for example, a variety of salmon somewhat fatter and larger than trout, out of which Gala prepared a delicious meal for us one evening, or the *golomyanka*, a scaleless fish so transparent that one can see the skeleton shimmering beneath its skin. These two fish, along with the sturgeon, are the most common species found in Lake Baykal.

The caviar sturgeon is indigenous to Lake Baykal and the Angara River. At certain times of the year the females are caught and released again after their eggs have been extracted with great care. Ten to twelve pounds of black caviar can be removed from each female annually without injuring the fish. Sturgeon is less delicate than salmon, which yields red caviar. The Angara, with its large volume of water, strong current, and relatively even temperature, provides an ideal environment for both.

We enjoyed the beautiful weather and were in high spirits. The lake was pure and clean as a mountain spring. Even Oleg demonstrated his respect for the water; he actually refrained from spitting into it. Of course, being addicted to this practice, along with most other Russians, he could not give it up entirely; but when he did spit, it was on the deck of the cutter.

104 *On the shores of Lake Baykal.* The shore is strewn with pebbles of every imaginable shape and color. I infected Oleg with my enthusiasm, and together we scoured the ground for especially beautiful specimens. My favorites were the thin pencil-shaped stones. Two large bags were soon filled with our colorful load. A storm rose in the evening of our third day. We looked for a cove that was shielded from the wind and moored the boat for the night.

Four days after we had left we were back in Listvyanka. The cost of our room and board was exceedingly modest. The crew absolutely refused to accept a tip. Apparently they, too, enjoyed our four-day expedition. We sped down the Angara in a "rocket", covering the 45 miles back to Irkutsk in less than an hour.

But what were we going to do with our rock collection weighing somewhere between 35 and 45 pounds? I suggested packing the collection in a crate and shipping it off to Moscow by rail. Oleg was afraid this would take too long and suggested sending it by air freight. With some trouble he managed to hunt up an old box, a hammer, and pliers. I bought a stack of newspapers in the hotel lobby to use as filling material. We carefully pulled the rusty nails out of the lid so that we could reuse them to nail the crate shut. We then took a taxi to the airport. The crate weighed 22 kilograms (48 pounds) and air freight cost almost one ruble per kilo, making a total of about $ 23. Oleg, who insisted on sharing the cost, also found this too expensive. So off we went back to town and railway station. We finally ended up paying almost as much anyway. The rail freight came to 13 rubles 50 kopeks; the taxi fares from hotel to airport, airport to railway station, and station to hotel again cost over 3 rubles; and since the box reached Moscow a few days ahead of us after all, we had to pay a storage fee of 3 rubles in order to get it out.

Yakutsk and the "Finger Rocks" Along the Lena River

We flew on to Yakutsk, capital of the Yakut Autonomous Soviet Socialist Republic. Almost one fourth of the more than 1 million square miles of this republic lies within the Arctic Circle. Temperatures run the extremes of an inland climate, from −94 °F in winter to 100 °F in summer. The entire region is closed to tourists.

The view below us was always the same: the endless taiga, that great expanse of forest which extends from the Urals to the Pacific, occasionally interrupted by a river with a few isolated settlements along its banks. Most of these colonies were founded in tsarist and postrevolutionary days. And more often than not, the founders were exiles — deportees and prisoners — who served their sentences in Siberia and stayed to populate this vast territory.

Our aircraft covered the 1,250 miles between Irkutsk and Yakutsk in three and a half hours. The plane was filled to the last seat. Many of the passengers were Yakuts, easily recognizable by their Mongolian features. Others came from western Russia, mostly younger people, who had committed themselves to work for some years on the development of Siberia's rich mineral resources as engineers, technicians, geologists, and surveyors. When the pilot announced over the loudspeaker that we were flying along the Lena, I was reminded of the Swiss professor, E. K. Weber, now over ninety years old and living in Zurich, who more than sixty years ago participated as geologist and astronomer in an expedition of the Academy of Sciences to the eastern Arctic Ocean. It had taken him eighteen days to journey from Irkutsk to Yakutsk along the mail route, most of which followed the ice on the frozen Lena. At that time a point on the coast of the Arctic Ocean south of Wrangel Island had been named Cape Weber by the tsarist authorities, but one no longer finds it on Soviet maps today.

Night had already fallen when we landed at the Yakutsk Airport.

Inside there was a jumble of waiting, chatting, sleeping people of every conceivable nationality; the smells of leather, bread, and fish mingled in the air — pioneer days and the jet age side by side.

105 *Defense tower of the former "wooden Kremlin" in Yakutsk.* When the cossacks founded the town in 1632, they erected a fortress, a wooden Kremlin, of which this tower was once a part. The contemporary wire sculpture belongs to an adjacent local museum, which houses many documents of Siberian settlement. Much of the exhibit also bears witness to the innumerable expeditions into the unknown which started out from Yakutsk.

106 *New buildings in Yakutsk.* Many of the streets have been torn up to lay pipelines for the natural gas that will be pumped up from the lower reaches of the Vulyuy River, a tributary of the Lena, to supply energy for industry and distant-heating systems.

107 *The Lenin Memorial on the main street in Yakutsk.*

108 *The director of the Linguistic Institute in Yakutsk.* On our tour of the Institute we made the acquaintance of Mrs. Yevdokia Korina, herself a Yakut, who is working on the study of the various Siberian language groups.

109 *Foundation of a house above the Siberian permafrost.* Yakutsk is the land of permafrost, where the ground never thaws below a depth of 3 feet. As a result, virtually every building is constructed on a foundation of wooden or concrete piles. Were the houses to rest directly on the frozen earth, their warmth would thaw the ground underneath, and they would eventually sink into the mire.

Although we had already obtained a visa in Moscow to visit Mirnyy, the Mirnyy authorities themselves canceled our permit without explanation. We made new plans. In the Yakutsk Mu-

МЫ НА В
— ПОСТРОЕ
ПОДГОТОВ
ВЫМ РАЗ
ОБЩЕСТВА

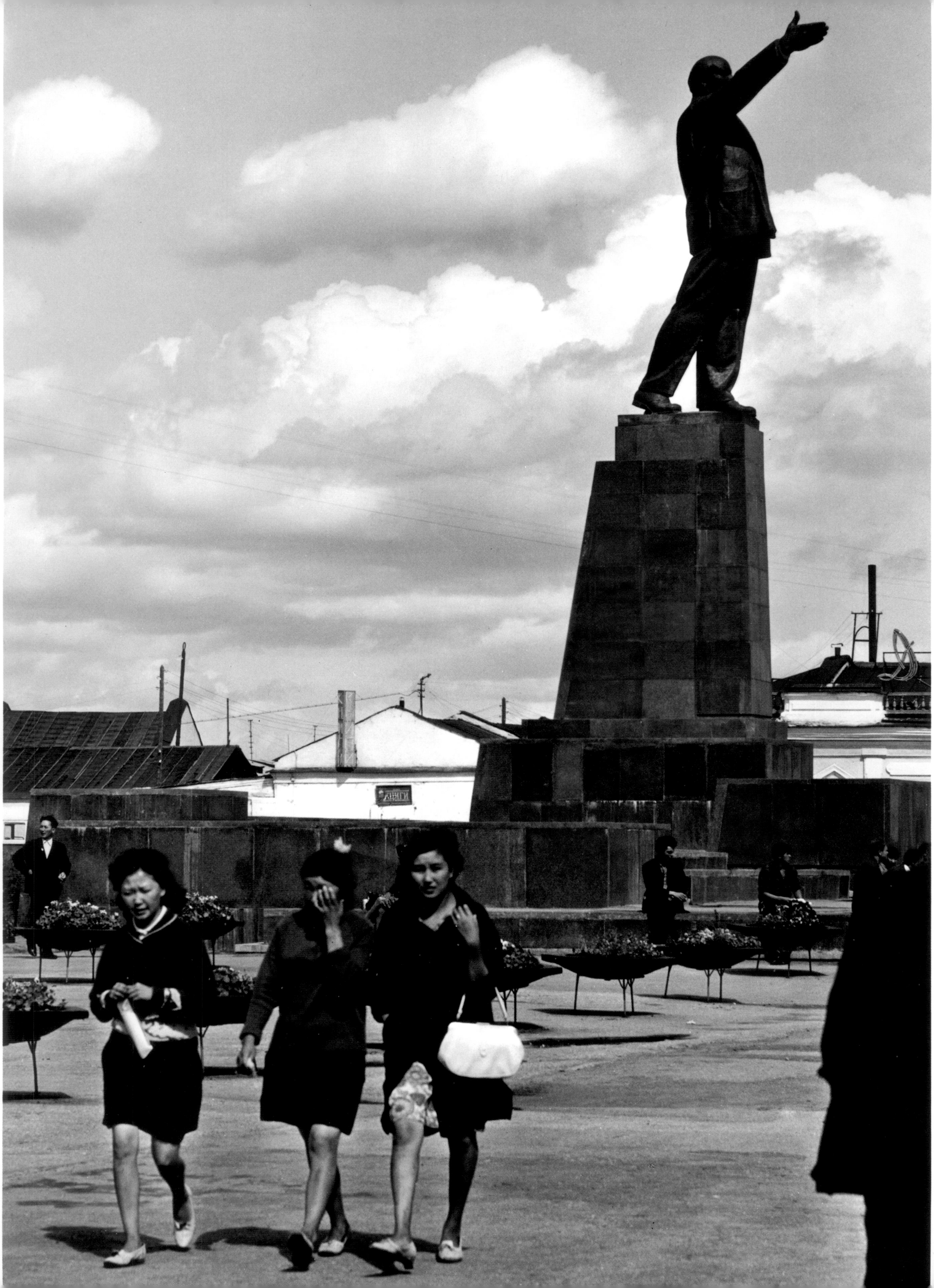
КНИГИ

110

111

seum I had come across a picture of a strange rock landscape situated some 180 miles upstream on the Lena. We now concentrated all our efforts on getting authorization for a boat trip up the river and were pleased that the director of the Yakutsk Marine Department supported our plan.

110 *Hydrofoil on the Lena.* We arrived at the dock in Yakutsk early in the morning and were surprised to find that this "rocket", with a capacity of 100 passengers had been put at our disposal. Oleg and I found ourselves in the excellent care of Captain Nikolai Larinov, mechanic Nikolai Avtayev, and stewardess Chentsova. We raced upstream at about 40 miles an hour.

The Lena, second-largest river in the Soviet Union, flows north almost 3,000 miles from its source near Lake Baykal into the Arctic Ocean, picking up numerous tributaries along the way. At several points the river is over 10 miles wide, so that one can barely see from one shore to the other. The exploration of the river is closely interwoven with the history of Siberian colonization; in 1878 the first European ship succeeded in reaching the broad delta of the Lena on the Arctic Ocean. Both banks of the river are rich in mineral resources such as coal, iron, copper, gold, and diamonds. Large fields of mammoth tusks have been unearthed in the delta.

The Yakut A.S.R., home of the Lena — what a vast territory! Its lands, its mineral wealth, its forests, and its water resources are simply immense. Yet up to now less than one percent of the area has been developed for agriculture. Of course, the difficulties in exploiting the territory's riches are imposing, and such problems as traffic and transport seem almost insurmountable. Nevertheless, a development program has been under way in recent years. Towns and settlements — as yet on no map — are springing up in the wilderness. Pipelines for oil and natural gas are under con-

struction. New lands are being tilled. Possibilities for shipping out the ores, precious metals, and diamonds are being explored. Naturally, all of this requires an immense concentration of men and materials. Here helicopter and airplane are indispensable tools for conquering the vast distances.

111 *The "finger rocks" on the Lena.* We saw the first of these curiously eroded rock formations after about four hours. The boat moored half an hour later, and Oleg and I were amply rewarded for our strenuous climb up the rocks by a magnificent panorama of the Lena River valley. We had to be back on board within two hours to allow time for the five-hour return journey.

112 *Cliffs on the shores of the Lena.* The bizarre cliffs bordering the river for several hundred miles are the remains of a Paleozoic sandstone plateau through which the river has carved its course for thousands and thousands of years. It was a perfectly calm day, and the weather was radiant; sky and water melted together on the horizon.

The Lena River calls to mind the name Vladimir Ilyich Lenin. From 1896 to 1899, Lenin was banished by the tsarist government to the village of Shushenskoye on the Yenisey River. The leaders of the revolution had all adopted pseudonyms to hide their identities: Molotov means "hammer", Stalin, "steel". Lenin named himself after the Lena.

By evening we were back in Yakutsk. The captain drove us to town in his car. To our surprise we did not have to pay a single kopek for the 375-mile journey. We had been guests of the Soviet government.

Oymyakon — Ust-Nera

We flew from Yakutsk to Ust-Nera with a stopover at Oymyakon. Oleg had purchased a pound of pears the previous evening, puny-looking ones that would probably not even be sold in a Swiss market. However, they were surprisingly tasty. They cost 2 rubles, 60 kopeks, almost $ 3.00.

The *Pravda* in which the pears had been wrapped contained an interesting article which I later had translated for me at our lodgings. A man from the Caucasus purchased 5,000 gladioli in his hometown. He paid 1,000 rubles for them, 20 kopeks apiece, packed them into light cartons, and flew them to the other end of the Soviet Union, to Verkhnekolymsk in the Siberian Far East. There in the barren tundra where no flowers grow and people earn well, he sold all of his 5,000 gladioli within twenty-four hours at 2 rubles apiece. His expenses amounted to some 800 rubles, leaving him a net profit of 9,200 rubles — that is, well over $ 10,000. Although similar occurrences are repeatedly denounced in the Soviet press, the state appears to do little to prevent such profiteering.

Pravda, the official organ of the Soviet Communist Party, is available in all the major cities of the Soviet Union. It is composed only once, however, in a central composing room in Moscow. Mats of the original pages are produced in the required number and flown out daily in all directions. After lead cuts have been made from the matrices in the respective cities, the paper is printed and appears, only slightly delayed.

113 *Near the airport in Oymyakon.* In Oymyakon we learned that we would be delayed two hours as the airport in Ust-Nera had been closed down by bad weather. We did some exploring near the landing strip. I was pleased with this unexpected delay. Oymyakon is the "cold pole" of the northern hemisphere, where a record temperature of −95.8 °F has been measured. Until a few

years ago Verkhoyansk, some 470 miles northwest of Oymyakon, had been the acknowledged cold pole. The area's wooden houses, exposed to such a severe climate, look far from sturdy; yet I am quite sure they are warm and comfortable inside. The inhabitants of the region undergo many inconveniences. When it rains in summer all paths and footways turn into ankle-deep mud.

114 *Greenhouse in Oymyakon.* With boards taken from old crates people construct their own little greenhouses, heating them with a stove to prolong the brief summer. Here they plant a few vegetables, cucumbers, and tomatoes. Since at the Arctic Circle fields cannot be sown until late May or early June, crops thus started are transplanted and are able to ripen in the few remaining summer months.

We reached Ust-Nera in the afternoon. Innokenty Cherkarov, editor of the local newspaper, the *Northern Sunrise* (circulation, 3,000), was there to meet us. We checked our luggage at the airport and flew on in a trusty old one-engine aircraft to the gold-mining settlement of Drashniy.

115 *The Draga, gold-extraction plant on the Indigirka River.* The Draga, a floating dredge, looms monster-like above the surface of the water. A conveyor belt (on the right) transports the gold-bearing deposits from the riverbed to the top of the structure along a system of sieves and nets which shake the metallic particles loose from the sludge. A second conveyor belt (on the left) returns the washed-out sludge to the river. The gold prospected in the area — several pounds a day — is stored under guard in a little wooden house known as the Trest. Once a week the yield is flown to Yakutsk and from there on to Moscow.

In Ust-Nera we lodged at a small, cozy boardinghouse, where we had a bedroom and a living room. There were now three of us;

Korneliy Alexeyevich Innokentyev, a fifty-one-year-old Yakut, had joined us in Yakutsk. He, too, was a journalist and worked for the *Soviet Yakutsk*. Since he had been in Merseburg, Germany during the war, he knew a few words of German; his pronunciation of "hands up" was excellent. I was fully aware that he had been sent along to keep an eye on me.

116 *Man with mushrooms in Ust-Nera.* Not only mushrooms, but also many berries, are to be found in late summer. We decided to go berrying. At the foot of a long sloping mountain, it struck me that it would be worth climbing up, not so much because of the bilberries, but because I wanted to reach a height at which I could finally photograph from above. Both journalists, though a good deal younger than we, soon gave up following us. I must say that in our low shoes we were poorly equipped for a trail that led up across swampy moors. Grassy hummocks—precarious stepping-stones—occasionally toppled under our weight, and we would find ourselves standing ankle-deep in mud.

117 *Valley of the Indigirka near Ust-Nera.* The laborious climb proved well worth the effort. Only from an altitude can one really see the landscape typical of this region, where taiga and tundra meet and only a rare, scraggly tree breaks the monotony.

We did not return until almost 9:30 P.M. Our prolonged absence had caused some concern. Innokenty told us that a few days before two men had been attacked by a bear in the same vicinity. The bear had succeeded in knocking the gun out of one of the men's hands and had killed the other, a relative of Innokenty's, the father of five children.

118 *Main street in Ust-Nera after a rain.* When it rains, the unpaved streets dissolve into lanes of deep mud. At first I hesitated to photograph the streets in this condition. But back at our boarding-

house again, I gave Korneliy a copy of my photographic volume *The Antarctic*, which he had long wanted to peruse in peace, and left him absorbed in the book while I went to mail a letter. On the way I made a long detour, during which I shot this picture. I was gone for almost two hours. Upon my return Korneliy was understandably annoyed and felt that he had been deceived. I really felt sorry for him; I had become quite fond of him. He was the only one who had consistently addressed me by my "full" name—Emil Emilyevich.

The poor condition of the roads in the provinces is repeatedly criticized in the Soviet press. In particular, it plays havoc with automobiles, and as a result, the Soviet Union has had to manufacture cars with more road clearance. The new Soviet-built Fiat, for example, is built much higher than its Italian counterpart.

Our clean, pleasant boardinghouse in Ust-Nera cost only 75 kopeks a night—less than a dollar and twenty-five times less than what I had paid for a room at the Rossiya in Moscow. However, the mosquitoes feasted on me again during the night.

Back in Yakutsk we were informed that my visas to the other Siberian places I had wished to visit had been canceled. Thus, we returned directly to Novosibirsk.

119 *Gold prospectors in the airplane.* Two other passengers were sitting with us in the small separate compartment to the rear of the Antonov. I had already noticed them at the airport in Yakutsk because they were rather unsteady on their feet. On the plane they finally both fell to snoring, and I could not even doze off because the one sitting behind me kept bumping his feet into my seat in his sleep. The moment they awoke, they pulled out a bottle of vodka. One of them wanted to give Oleg an unopened bottle, but he refused. When the same fellow, slightly inebriated but very likable, turned all his charm on me, I had no choice but

to accept the gift. Oleg struck up a conversation with them. They had come directly from Magadan, a gold-prospecting location. Vassiliy Udovenko (on the left) had given up his prospecting job to work as a driver and was now flying home on holiday. The other, Ivan Yegorovich, thirty-eight years old, belonged to an *artels*, a collective of gold prospectors. The government encourages adventurous young men with strong constitutions to dig for gold on their own in areas allotted to them for this purpose. When they have proved themselves "worthy of a concession", they can rent the necessary tools and machinery, such as bulldozers. Ivan, who was almost sober again, described his life as a gold prospector. The building of the living quarters for the twenty members of the *artels* had begun in January, a very difficult undertaking, since the prospecting location was near the cold pole. Construction work did not stop until temperatures had dropped to −67 °F. The actual gold-digging season ran from March to August. The men worked extremely hard, usually twenty hours a day, to prospect as much gold and thus earn as much as possible. Ivan apologized for having drunk too much. The season had just ended, and he had not tasted a drop of alcohol for eight months, since its consumption was strictly forbidden in the *artels*. If a prospector lost one day's work because of excessive drinking, five days were deducted, and if it happened again, he was expelled from the *artels*. But now Ivan was on his way home to Alma-Ata, where he had a house, wife, and daughter. Since his wife, a teacher, did not appreciate his drinking at home either, he could indulge only while he was traveling. His *artels* had had a very good season; the men had each earned about 8,000 rubles (almost $ 9,000). We ran into both men again at the airport in Novosibirsk while we were waiting for our connection to Moscow. They had another bottle with them and cheerfully waved to us.

Siberian Winter

By now I had traveled to the U.S.S.R. six times. But I simply could not imagine a photographic volume of the Soviet Union without a section on winter in Siberia. In addition, I had set my hopes on visiting Boguchany in the spring to witness the ice breakup on the Angara River.

In mid-January I was notified by telephone that I should be ready to leave within the next few days. Although I could get no further details, I gathered from replies to my questions that we were going to head toward the Arctic. I immediately set everything in motion to get a visa. To condition myself for the cold, I wore only tropical suits in the Swiss winter. My Leica equipment was ready; it had been winterized long before. Two days later another call came from Moscow—the plans had fallen through. They would get in touch with me again at the beginning of February.

I had become accustomed to frustration. However, when I still had heard nothing by mid-February, I began to get anxious. Finally, at the beginning of March, I was able to begin. I arrived in Moscow equipped with a good supply of warm underclothes, the warmest fur-lined boots available in Switzerland, and a fur-lined jacket. In Moscow I purchased a practical Russian fur cap with earflaps to complete my wardrobe. But all hopes of combining this journey with side trips to the Arctic Ocean were dashed. I even encountered skepticism regarding permission to visit Boguchany. No explanations were forthcoming. Officials just shrugged their shoulders in response to my inquiries. I was even more disappointed, however, when I learned that Oleg would not be available to accompany me. Inna, an interpreter, was to be my new companion.

Yakutsk, –47 °F

Our first destination was Yakutsk again. Before landing the plane the captain announced the ground temperature — minus 38 °F! This was the first piece of good news in a long time; I had already feared that I would be too late for the real "Siberian temperatures". Yuri Semyonov, a correspondent, and Victor Yakovlev, a Yakut newspaper photographer, met us at the airport. On our way to the Lena Hotel, Yuri informed us that it had not been nearly so cold the day before — only –5°.

The next morning the temperature read –47°. Since I was already familiar with the town, I set out unaccompanied before sunrise to take some photographs in the brittle cold. I would like to describe how I dressed to ward off the cold: first regular undershorts, then three pairs of "long johns"; over this the pants of my pajamas and a pair of corduroy trousers; a short-sleeved and a long-sleeved undershirt, a knitted shirt, a heavy sweater, and my fur-lined jacket; on my feet nylon socks, thick woolen knee socks, and the fur-lined boots; on my hands a pair of thin silk gloves, then woolen gloves open at the finger tips — they had stood the test during my expedition in the Antarctic and give me freedom of movement to handle the cameras — and fur-lined mittens hanging around my neck; finally my two Leicas and four lenses, all of which I tucked away for protection under my jacket. Lastly I put on the fur cap and pulled the flaps down over my ears. Shapeless as a barrel, I clumped off into the outside world. The sudden cold hit me in the face like a fist.

120 *Lenin Prospect in Yakutsk.* Eerie billowing clouds of vapor trailed behind the vehicles. The people, too, hurrying along heavily muffled, were enveloped in fog. Out of the chimneys climbed columns of smoke which hovered above the city in the golden rays of the rising sun. I was surprised to discover that the cold can be visible in such attractive shapes and colors.

The snow was incredibly dry, as fine as flour, and crunched under my boots. The cold stung my skin. I was reminded of something Professor Weber once wrote: "At 5 below zero the snow crunches underfoot, at 45 below exhaling makes a rushing sound, and we knew that it had to be about 75 below when our spit turned into a little ball of ice and rolled away over the ground...."

121 *House in Yakutsk shortly after sunrise.* Where the warmth from the heated houses escapes through the windows, fantastic ice formations take shape in the cold. Newer buildings are fitted with triple-paned windows.

122 *Natural gas for Yakutsk.* The streets have been torn up to lay pipelines for natural gas. In order to thaw the earth, barrels of oil are lined up on their sides and set on fire. They burn for many hours, sometimes even for days, until the ground is soft enough to start digging. Workers and pedestrians warm themselves at the flames.

123 *Protective cover on the engine of a motor vehicle.* Starting an engine in this murderous climate is quite a challenge. A thick quilted cover is tied around the hoods of vehicles. Once the motor has been started, it is left running even over long waiting periods.

124 *Early morning sun in the streets of Yakutsk.* A sunrise at 47 below is unforgettable; what a delicate contrast between warm and cold colors. I felt more comfortable in Siberia in winter than in summer. Now there were no mosquitoes to make my life miserable. However, there is a price to pay, at least for those who are determined to record their experiences on film. It was agony to work with the cameras in thin silk gloves. My fingers were frozen stiff, and the skin on my finger tips cracked in the cold. It was painful to come into contact with the metal on the cameras when I was changing the film. My fingernails, too, were so brittle that

125

124

they kept breaking off. Had it been any colder, handling the cameras would probably have been altogether impossible.

125 *Boys' ice hockey rink in Yakutsk.*

126 *Staircase on the Lenin Prospect in Yakutsk.* Yuri was acquainted with an ivory carver whose studio was on the third floor of a building on the Lenin Prospect. Climbing up to visit him, Yuri hurried up the stairs, looking neither right nor left, as if there were nothing special to see. I, however, was so fascinated by the ice-encrusted staircase that I almost forgot our visit.

127 *Ammossov Terenti, ivory carver, in Yakutsk.* Only a door separated the well-heated studio from the "glaciated" staircase. Ammossov, a friendly fifty-eight-year-old Yakut "bear", showed me some of his beautiful carvings: a large chess game, for example, and an interesting replica of the Kremlin in Yakutsk. But most interesting was the material he used—mammoth tusks. Thousands have been unearthed in the Siberian permafrost where ice blocks dating back to the ice age are still being excavated. Not only have perfectly preserved skeletons of mammoths been found, but also fur-covered animals, whose meat—frozen underground for millions of years—has even been fed to dogs.

128 *Ice cream on the Lenin Prospect in Yakutsk.* Even at 40 below zero these young ladies cannot resist the pleasures of an ice cream cone.

129 *Marina Dogdanova, schoolgirl in Yakutsk.* In the Soviet Union children were formerly required to attend school for eight years: four years of primary school and four years of secondary school. Two further years of college preparatory work were originally voluntary but have now been added to the compulsory school curriculum.

130 *Construction of pipelines for natural gas in Yakutsk.* The drilling and processing of natural gas is one of Russia's youngest industries. The seemingly inexhaustible supply not only serves millions of households but also drives turbines for the production of electricity.

131 *New structures at the thermoelectric plant in Yakutsk.* Although it turned bitterly cold toward evening, the men were still hard at work, hammering, riveting, and welding. It is incomprehensible how they can continue working outside in such cold; construction is not halted until temperatures sink to $-58°$.

The thermoelectric plant in Yakutsk, fed by natural gas, is already in partial operation. The exploitation of natural gas in the Soviet Union has made tremendous strides. By the end of 1970 over 50 percent of the urban and 20 percent of the rural population was expected to be supplied with natural gas. Exports are also flourishing: contracts for delivery have been signed with Czechoslovakia, the German Democratic Republic, Austria, Italy, and the German Federal Republic. Since 1958, Russian natural gas has been flowing through pipelines across the border into Austria, gateway to the Western European market. According to Soviet data, deliveries to Western Europe should reach 13 billion standard *cubic meters* (Nm³) annually by 1975.

Aldan

We flew from Yakutsk to Aldan in an Ilyushin 14. Every seat was taken. Since the entrance to the airplane had been left open for quite some time—the outside temperature was still about −40—it was frightfully cold in the cabin. It took a good half hour to warm up. In two hours we arrived at Aldan, some 250 miles southwest of Yakutsk. From the plane I noticed that there was still a great deal of snow on the ground, much more than in Yakutsk. Lida Tolmachova, an employee of the local newspaper, met the four of us—Inna, Yuri, Victor, and me—at the little airport on the outskirts of the city and took us to a small inn.

Aldan was founded in 1922, when 500 young people began prospecting for gold in the Aldan River, a tributary of the Lena. The population is already more than 20,000; most of the people here live "off the gold". The area around the Aldan and Indigirka rivers has become one of the most important gold-prospecting centers in the Yakut A.S.S.R. Life is not bad here. People earn well, and a monthly income four times higher than in Moscow is not unusual. Furthermore, workers are granted six months' paid leave every three years, during which the gold prospectors and their families can fly to warmer places in the southern Soviet Union.

132 *Two little boys on their way to school in Aldan.* The sun broke through the haze only for a short time in the morning. The rest of the day a fine mist covered the valley, and the landscape was bathed in a diffuse light.

133 *One of the main streets in Aldan.* Aldan is a typical Siberian settlement, in which most of the houses are built of wood. The town lies nestled in a hollow. A polytechnic institute is under construction on the northern slopes. Food processing, a wholesale bakery, a brewery, and chicken farms are the principal enterprises here.

134 *Mother and child coming home from shopping.* I thoroughly enjoyed life in the Siberian winter. The people, whose existence entails a never-ending struggle against nature, are extremely open and friendly to strangers.

It was no longer so cold in Aldan, "only" −14°. The temperatures here range from 49 below in winter to 104 above in summer. During the spring seedlings are cultivated in small greenhouses; at the end of May, they are transplanted to the fields. Potatoes, cabbage, cucumbers, tomatoes, and even melons can ripen during the short but intense summer.

135 *Man cutting wood.* While walking about the town, I came across this man who was cutting firewood with a power saw. Although wood is still the most common fuel, natural gas will probably replace it in the near future.

Our hotel, also an older wooden structure, did not have all the conveniences, but the atmosphere was homely and pleasant. In the bathroom stood a few barrels of water from which one ladled the quantity required into a basin hanging on the wall. There was a kind of valve underneath which one pressed to get running water.
The toilet was quite another story. It consisted of an open wooden shed about fifty paces from the hotel. The front entrance was "hers", the rear "his". Apparently, many men had not made the effort to go all the way around to the rear of the outhouse; as a result a yellowish-brown glacier, interspersed with various pop-art shapes, had formed in front, which was rather treacherous in the darkness of night.

Early in the morning we drove off in a jeep with Nikolai Danilovich Afonin, manager of the Aldanskiy Kolkhoz, to visit reindeer breeders about 50 miles south of Aldan. The road,

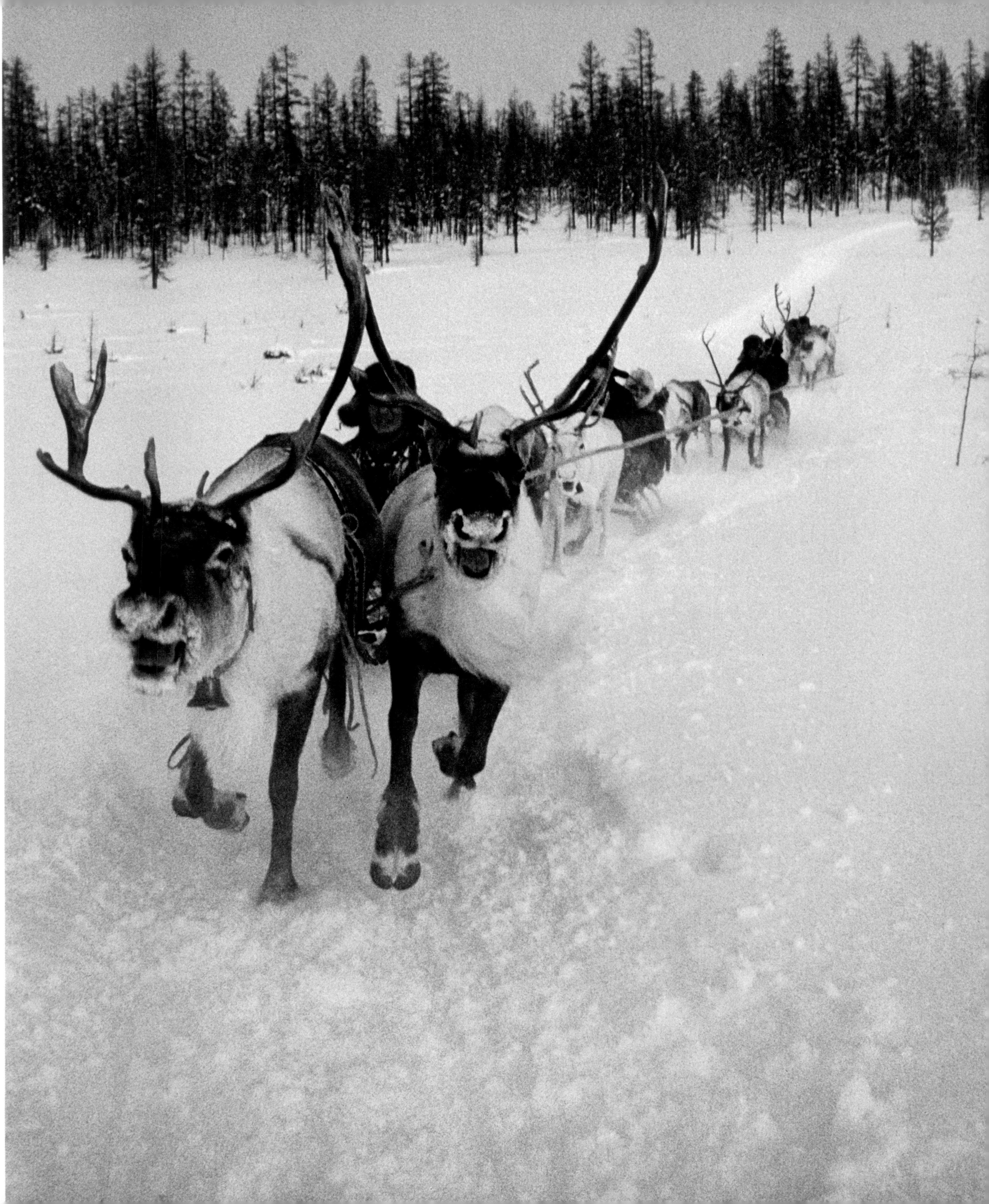

stretches of which were paved and cleared of snow, leads north to Yakutsk and south over the passes of the Stanovoy Mountains to Bolshoy Never, a station on the Trans-Siberian Railway. When we stopped and got out, we arranged with the driver to pick us up on his return in the evening. We trudged through the snow-covered taiga for half an hour until we reached the settlement.

136 *Reindeer breeders' settlement of the Aldanskiy Kolkhoz.* Most of the families live in tents which can be comfortably heated even in extreme cold. Antlers were lying about in the snow, skins were hung up to dry, some reindeer stood nearby in enclosures—a unique setting. The herd was still between one and two hours away and was being driven toward the camp. We were invited into a log cabin where *babushka*, father, mother, and son welcomed us. And what a feast was set before us: reindeer roast, liver, kidneys, and heart; sweets for dessert; and, of course, one large glass of vodka after another, each of which had to be downed in one shot. Although the vodka still set my throat on fire, I was beginning to acquire a taste for it. After the meal a train of sleighs was made ready to ride out and meet the herd. My boots were considered inadequate for the ride in the open; I was given a pair lined with thick fur, such as the herdsmen themselves wear.

137 *Reindeer in a corral.* A few reindeer are kept separate from the herd for use as draft animals.

138 *Reindeer breeder from the Aldanskiy Kolkhoz.* This man drove the sleigh in which I was seated. Each of the six sleighs was drawn by a team of reindeer. At full gallop we wound through the forest in the stinging cold, reaching the vicinity of the herd in a good half hour. Unfortunately, I could not make the shot I had hoped for, since we were not on an open field, but rather in the middle of the taiga, through which the animals were being driven in smaller separated groups.

139 *Sleigh ride on the way back to the colony.* This time I sat in the lead sleigh, turned so that I could see all the others behind me. It was no simple matter to take pictures as we raced through the countryside. I had to hang on for dear life, so as not to be thrown clear of the sleigh and then try to manage the cameras as well. The violent jerky motion of the ride made it well-nigh impossible to focus a shot. In addition, the vodka, which kept me immune to the cold, also left me pleasantly euphoric. I do not think I have ever felt happier and more peaceful during all my travels in other countries or continents than I did during that sleigh ride with the Yakut reindeer herdsmen.

We drove back to Aldan in high spirits. My companions sang loud and long—melodious, melancholy songs—and I joined in enthusiastically. Fortunately, the driver himself was perfectly sober for the trip through the dark night. Yuri had him stop at a small store to buy still another bottle. Before climbing into the jeep again, we had to clink glasses and down the contents. That was no vodka, but something much more powerful. I staggered into the jeep. Although I did my level best to pull myself together, I was soon forced to capitulate. Several hours later I awoke, lying fully dressed on the bed in my hotel room. Yuri afterward confessed that he had bought pure alcohol.

Lena — Baykal — Irkutsk

At six o'clock in the morning there was a knock on the door of our room in Aldan. It was Inna, asking us to pack right away since the car would be there at seven to take us to the airport. "Why to the airport?" I asked. "We are flying back to Yakutsk." "But that's impossible. I need at least one more full day in Aldan," I replied. "No," said Inna, "we are flying back to Yakutsk this morning. You've already seen what there is to see. You've photographed reindeer and taken pictures in Aldan, that's enough. ..." I was completely taken aback; this tone of voice was new to me. Had I flown more than 5,600 miles to Siberia only to be ordered to turn on my heels and go right back to Moscow? For the first time in all my travels through the U.S.S.R., I lost my temper. I refused to pack. I still wanted to photograph the bread-making process at the bakery, for instance, and to visit some more Yakut families. It was no use; we had to fly back to Yakutsk. And when, on top of all this, the sun rose blood red on the horizon, heralding a sparkling sunny day, I felt as if I had been robbed.

Once more in Yakutsk I was determined to take advantage of the beautiful weather. We rented a car to visit the settlement of Maya on the opposite bank of the Lena about 25 miles away. It was still 40 below zero. We reached the river in about half an hour.

140 *"Road" across the frozen Lena in Yakutsk.* The ice — blue and clear — was about 8 feet thick. Since the river was between 2 to 3 miles wide at this point and only one lane crossed the ice, turn-outs had been cleared as well. The traffic signs in the middle of nowhere looked positively absurd.
I got out here and there to take shots of the "ice street". The cold seemed even more intense on this vast armor of ice. It immediately penetrated the thick soles of my shoes and crept up into my fur-lined jacket so that I was glad to climb into the heated car again. I had to keep wiping the steam off my glasses, but I stowed my

cameras in the trunk of the car where it was so cold that the lenses did not cloud over. As we approached the north bank of the Lena, the driver picked up speed to get up the steep embankment onto the street.

141 *Village of Bestyakh on the Lena.* The small settlement lies huddled at the foot of the embankment and looks out upon the vast river landscape carpeted with snow.
I climbed up the steep slope to photograph some children who had made themselves a slide in the snow. Yuri kept shouting something at them from below. Soon I realized that he was trying to make them laugh. Apparently, Soviet journalists and photographers are urged to take pictures of laughing children. This is probably why one sees so many laughing faces in Soviet magazines. The children at the Lena were having so much fun that they certainly did not need to be coaxed into merriment.

142 *Man with the blocks of ice.* In Maya, a typical Siberian village, I discovered this man transporting blocks of ice, which he had sawed out of the frozen Lena, to a wooden shed where he lowered them into a pit about 10 feet deep. The ground here is permanently frozen below 3 feet in depth, and the ice never melts, even during the brief hot summer. Thus, he had a perfect freezer. This is a Siberian custom of many centuries' standing.

143 *Member of the Lenin Kolkhoz in Maya.* We came across this rider
144 on his shaggy Siberian horse. He took us to the stables of the Lenin Kolkhoz, a collective of horse breeders. Great care is required to keep horses near the cold pole as the enormous change of temperature between the warm stables and the open air is very dangerous for the animals; only an extremely hardy breed can withstand the severe climatic conditions.

Yuri gave a magnificent farewell dinner on the evening before

144

146

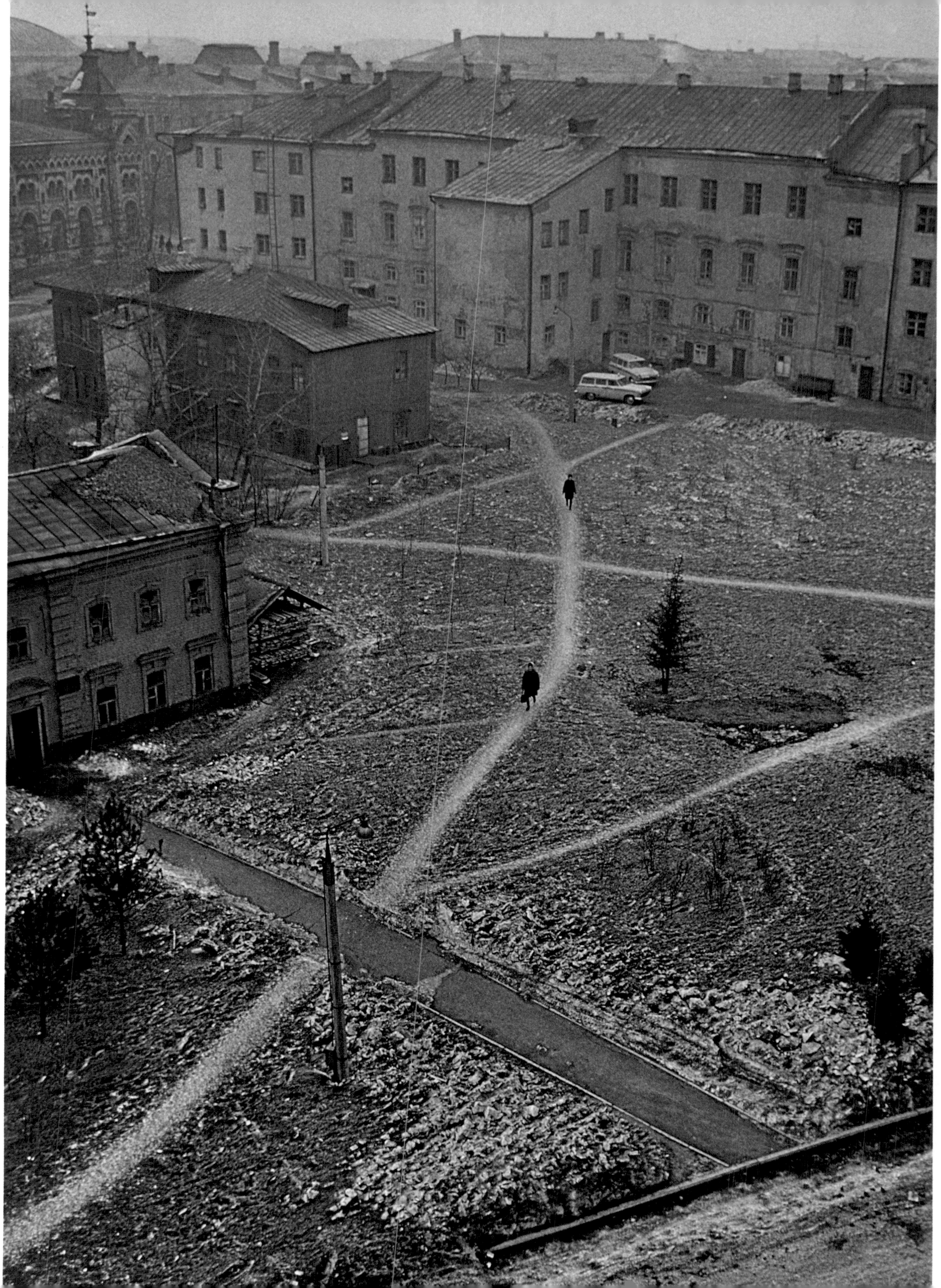

our return to Irkutsk: thin slices of frozen fish as an appetizer followed by *pelmeny*, a dish similar to ravioli, cucumbers, hot-house scallions, horse meat, peas, ham, lemonade, and three bottles of cognac for four people. The fourth member of our circle was a radio correspondent, who was planning to drive a jeep from here to Magadan. He hoped to cover the distance in ten days. How I envied him! We drank a toast to a project which I suggested — traversing the entire Soviet Union together in jeeps, from west to east, from the Baltic Sea to Vladivostok. "Tomorrow, tomorrow," Yuri kept saying in English. "Maybe."

145 *"Black snow" in Irkutsk.* What a shock, after the pristine white landscape at the Lena, to plod through the hideous gray-black snow here in Irkutsk, soiled by the sooty smoke from thousands of chimneys. Now Inna finally understood my outburst in Aldan when I was refused another day to carry out my plans.

On the plane to Irkutsk I had decided to drive to Lake Baykal again. Having seen the extraordinary beauty of the lake in summer, I was especially eager to revisit the magnificent expanse of water and the surrounding landscape in its winter finery.
We rented a car and drove to Lake Baykal in beautiful weather. The road, cleared of snow, was in good condition even in winter, but we had to drive for over 12 miles before the ugly black soot that had been on the snow in and around Irkutsk finally disappeared altogether. After one and a half hours we reached the spot near Listvyanka where the Angara flows out of Lake Baykal.

146 *Outlet of the Angara on Lake Baykal.* Two women, visible as two small dots in the picture, were walking across the lake from the opposite shore to go shopping in Listvyanka. Where the waters of lake and river meet, the solid layer of ice suddenly disintegrates. For a certain distance downstream from its outlet, the Angara never freezes over even in the lowest temperatures. Because of its

enormous depth Lake Baykal has a constant temperature of 39 °F above zero. Therefore, the water passing from the frozen lake into the fast current must flow a certain distance to cool off before it can freeze over.

147 *On the shores of frozen Lake Baykal.* Blocks of ice, at times extraordinarily translucent, were heaped along the shore. Beyond them one could see the endless expanse of the Baykal still covered, in mid-March, with 6 feet of solid ice. The sun, however, was gaining strength; patches of earth were already visible along the shore.

148 *Siberian winter draws to a close.* On the day of my departure to Moscow, I saw the sun rise on the Siberian horizon for the last time. The higher it rose, the faster it melted the thick lacy ice patterns which had formed overnight on my hotel window. Spring, however, was already in the air. In a few weeks the mighty roaring of the breakup on lakes and rivers would resound in the air.

In Moscow I made one last effort to obtain permission to visit the Angara near Boguchany in May to witness the ice breakup — if possible together with Dr. von Stackelberg. Once again I waited in vain. It had always been my intention to conclude this volume with photographs of the ice breakup, the symbol of approaching spring. Since this must remain an unfulfilled dream, I close the description of my travels with a passage from Traugott von Stackelberg's first book, "Beloved Siberia", about the land to which he had been banished by the tsarist government. He wrote: "I was awakened on the 6th of May toward 3 A.M. by a mighty sound. Outside a muffled thunderous rumbling and hissing filled the air, with great shuddering crashes in between. That could only be the breakup. I dressed quickly and ran to the schoolyard, from which I was able to overlook the river stretching east and west to the horizon. Yes, the ice had broken and was pushing west. Great floes passed each other in the gurgling black waters. Suddenly in the middle of the river, where the island was, an iceberg reared up out of the water, high as a church tower and wide as a marketplace. Other islands of ice three feet thick crashed into this mountain with tremendous force and were then lifted into the air as if by some mysterious power. They shoved against each other, piled on top of each other, rose towering into the air, and finally came crashing down into the turbulent waters again. I was so overwhelmed by the drama of this spectacle, which seemed to me the embodiment of primeval chaos, that I had not noticed Olga standing beside me. We were alone, for it was still very early. The sky gradually became suffused with a luminous pink, which was reflected in the jagged aquamarine icebergs. Then the icebergs seemed to roll on. They rose threateningly and fell booming back into the dark tide, plunged beneath the waves and reappeared, turned and reared up again. The water washed over some of the great blocks, sweeping them downstream with unbelievable speed. Suddenly the movement slowed, the water rose, and the approaching floes slid onto each other. Further down at the foothills, the Boguchan, the ice had created a barrier. The Angara was 2 miles wide at our level, at the Boguchan and beyond it widened to 8 ½ miles. Water and ice rose higher and higher as they came ever closer. Then the gigantic gray and pink mass began to shudder; it roared and hissed. The water had found a way through and now came roaring down toward its natural bed again, while on the river bank great cakes of ice piled up to a height of 33 feet. We were both so absorbed in this drama of natural forces that we spoke not a word. Then warm sunshine bathed the white walls of the church in light, silhouetting its malachite-green bulbous spires against the purple-gray sky in the west."

Emil Schulthess

Acknowledgments

Baron Traugott von Stackelberg, whose interest in the realization of the present volume has already been mentioned, was unfortunately no longer able to witness its publication; he died on November 8, 1970, at the age of seventy-nine.

I am particularly indebted to Ambassador August Lindt, Counselor of Embassy Olivier Exchaquet, Embassy Secretary Francis Pianca, and the entire staff of the Swiss Embassy in Moscow for their support in the planning and execution of this volume. Among the many who each in his way contributed to the creation of this book, I wish especially to mention the following: Jeanpierre Allemann, Bern; Alfred Boch, New York; Rudolf Bützberger, Zurich; Howard Chapnick, New York; Ernst and Rudolf Debrunner, Zurich; Albert R. Diener, Zurich; Dr. h. c. Henri Dumur, Wetzlar; Professor Dr. Emil Egli, Zurich; Eduard Fahrni, Meilen; Hans Frei, Zurich; Heinz Gebhardt, Dielsdorf; Fritz Girardin, Zurich; Walter Glättli, Stäfa; Professor Dr. Heini Hediger, Zurich; Fritz Hofer, Zurich; Franz Hörburger, Zurich; Ambassador Hans Keller, Belgrade; Konrad Kyburz, Dielsdorf; Theo Kisselbach, Wetzlar; Erwin Landert, Steinmaur; Adolf Lemans, Zurich; Robert Lienhard, Neerach; Dr. Dieter Lutz, Munich; Professor Dr. Fritz Müller, Zurich; Hans E. Müller, Dielsdorf; Hansruedi Müller, Kloten; Ingrid Parge, Zurich; Willy Petraglio, Biel; Heinz Sorgatz, Zurich; Alois Stutz, Bremgarten; August Voegele, Kloten; Bruno Vögeli, Dielsdorf; Professor Ernst K. Weber, Zurich; Dr. med. Josef Wiederkehr, Zurich; Ambassador Alfred Zehnder, Zurich; Max Zimmerli, Basel; Constantin Zuppiger, Zurich.

Photographic expeditions to the U. S. S. R. should be most carefully considered and technically very well-prepared. Not only is it impossible to obtain accessories and parts for Western-made camera equipment, but one also looks in vain for film material such as Kodachrome, which was used for the color photographs reproduced here. My equipment consisted of two Leicaflex and four Leica M-4 cameras as well as Leitz lenses with focal lengths varying from 21 to 400 millimeters. The equipment had to withstand severe climatic conditions and excessive wear and tear. Neither the extreme temperatures, as low as −47 °F in Siberia, nor the merciless treatment occasioned by being shipped with every conceivable mode of transportation ever led to the failure of any of this Leitz equipment.

Forch–Zurich, Autumn 1971   Emil Schulthess

Table of Contents